MW01620339

Yakima Valley MEMORIES

THE EARLY YEARS

Presented by

ACKNOWLEDGMENTS

The Yakima Herald-Republic, the Yakima Valley Museum, and the Yakima Valley Regional Library are pleased to present "Yakima Valley Memories." This unique pictorial book is not a publication of just these three entities, however. It is the result of contributions made by many people and organizations from throughout the Yakima Valley.

We are all indebted, first of all, to those early Valley residents who captured their time – our history – in photographs, and provided us with a glimpse into their lives. And, secondly, all Valley residents are indebted to the organizations and individuals who are committed to preserving our history in archives and personal collections.

In addition to the generous contributions of both time and photo archives from the Yakima Valley Museum and the Yakima Valley Regional Library, we also received valuable assistance and photos from the numerous Herald-Republic readers who took the time to share their photos and stories.

We are also indebted to **Yakima Federal Savings & Loan,** which published one of the first books of historic images on the Yakima Valley as part of its contribution to America's Bicentennial in 1976.

Historical information for the chapter essays came from:

- "History of the Yakima Valley" (by Professor W.D. Lyman, 1919)
- "Yakima: A Centennial Perspective 1885-1985" (Jim Newbill & Herb Blisard, editors)
- "Yakima: A Centennial Reflection 1885-1985" (by George M. Martin, Paul Schafer and William E. Scofield)
- "Yakima Jubilee 1885-1960" (by Click Relander and George M. Martin)
- Yakima Herald-Republic archives

 • ISBN: 1-932129-91-X

Published by Pediment Publishing, a division of The Pediment Group, Inc. www.pediment.com Printed in Canada

Contents

Above: Hauling plums to warehouse from the Olson Ranch, Parker Bottom, August 15, 1909. *Yakima Valley Museum*

Foreword

At almost the same time Ka-mi-akin of the Yakamas was introducing the Catholic "black robes" to his Yakima Valley, a British sculptor named Frederick Scott Archer was introducing a photographic process that would eventually allow intrepid travelers to carry cameras into the remote West.

Ka-mi-akin would represent the people who lived in the Valley before the arrival of Europeans; the camera would capture the images of those who would come later.

And the Catholic priests who founded the mission at Ahtanum were just the first of those who would come.

This book is dedicated to all those who were here and those who have arrived in succeeding generations.

This joint project of the Yakima Herald-Republic, the Yakima Valley Regional Library, and the Yakima Valley Museum is intended to give a kaleidoscope look back at the years from roughly 1890 through 1939. The photos that fill these pages offer a snapshot, if you will, of the lives and times of our communities in those years.

For they were interesting times — from the frontier celebrations of statehood in 1889, the massive expansion of agriculture and the dramatic transition from "horse-and-buggy travel" to the Age of the Automobile, with a couple of presidential visits thrown in for good measure. We have tried to capture some of the biggest occasions while focusing, too, on those smaller events that shape every day life.

We have to believe that Ka-mi-akin and the original Catholic fathers could never have imagined where their meeting would lead. Just as we have to imagine that Frederick Archer could never have imagined how grateful we would be that today we have photographic images to teach us about our past.

CHAPTER ONE

Views Around the Valley

With the advent of more affordable and portable photography equipment around the last quarter of the 19th century, proud civic leaders and landowners wanted to capture the panoramic vistas they called home. There were many to be found in the Yakima Valley.

Over that century and into this one, those panoramas and cityscapes would show new generations just how the Yakima Valley had changed in the ensuing years.

Street scenes from cities and towns through the Valley — what was first called North Yakima and later Yakima, what was first called Yakima City and later Union Gap, plus Toppenish, Grandview, Prosser, Buena and Sunnyside — all show the growth from rural gathering places to bustling commercial centers. And in some of those communities today, the trend has been back toward what used to be.

Left: View from the banks of the Yakima River at Prosser, circa 1910. *Yakima Valley Museum*

Right: View of North Yakima, early 1900s. Center left is the Public Library that was built in 1906. *Yakima Valley Museum*

Above: View of Eighth and Yakima avenues, looking east, North Yakima, 1903. *Yakima Valley Museum*

Right: View from Chestnut Street North through alley to a crowded Yakima Avenue, North Yakima, circa 1901. (Also note hose cart shed for fireman). *Jack Whitnall Collection, Frank Lanterman, photographer*

Below: A view of Yakima City (now Union Gap), circa 1884. The white building is Yakima City courthouse. It was moved to North Yakima in 1885. *Yakima Valley Museum*

Above: View of Yakima looking toward Selah Gap, early 1900s. The old First Presbyterian Church in the foreground, Court House in the center and the library to the right of the Presbyterian Church. *Yakima Valley Museum*

Left: A view of Main Street in downtown Prosser, circa 1907. *Yakima Valley Museum*

Below: Street scene in Yakima City with First National Bank on left side of photograph, circa 1882. *Yakima Valley Museum*

Above Left: A view looking east down Yakima Avenue, North Yakima, circa 1908. *Yakima Valley Museum*

Above Right: A view of Yakima Avenue, circa 1910. Lund Building, built in 1889 on left corner of Yakima Avenue, North Yakima. *Yakima Valley Museum*

Right: A view of the northwest corner of Division and South Second streets in Grandview, circa 1911. *Bleyhl Community Library, Grandview*

Left: Bird's-eye view of Yakima Avenue looking west from Third Street, Yakima, circa 1918.

Yakima Valley Museum

Below: View of Toppenish business center, circa 1915.

Yakima Valley Museum

YAKIMA

Above: An aerial view of the Selah Valley looking South, circa 1920. The Yakima River is in foreground. *Yakima Valley Museum*

Left: Yakima street scene, looking west from Third Street and Yakima Avenue, North Yakima, circa 1910. Notice the cars, horses, buggies and trolley tracks. You can see two of the four clocks that had been installed on Yakima Avenue. *Yakima Valley Museum*

Right: Yakima Avenue, Yakima, circa 1922. Hotel Yakima in the lower left corner. *Yakima Valley Museum*

Right: Street scene in Sunnyside, circa 1927. *Yakima Valley Museum*

Below Right: View of Yakima Avenue at night, Yakima, circa 1938. Neon signs for Liberty Theater and Commercial Hotel on the south side of the street. *John Pigion*

Below: Street scene in Buena, circa 1935. *Yakima Valley Museum. Dorothea Lange, photographer*

Above: Yakima Avenue looking east from First Street, Yakima, circa 1930. *Yakima Valley Museum*

CHAPTER TWO

PLANES, TRAINS & AUTOMOBILES

The history of settlers in the Yakima Valley is inextricably tied to the Northern Pacific Railroad. The railroad had as its goal a line that ran from Lake Superior to the Puget Sound, and on December 23, 1884, Yakima City became its westernmost outpost.

In fact, it was Northern Pacific that coerced the businesses of Yakima City to move four miles to be near the depot at what was then called North Yakima. The company offered free land in the vicinity of the new depot — in reality an empty boxcar until a wooden building could be built on Front Street — to any business that would move (building and all) from the older town that would eventually be renamed Union Gap.

Within a generation, another kind of train had come to Yakima. Trolleys were a thriving business by 1910. Though trolleys remained in service until 1947, the beginning of the decline of this service was marked by the development of consumer-priced automobiles in the 1920s.

Commercial aircraft were also being developed after the end of World War I, with passenger flights available at the Yakima Airport beginning in 1928 — the same year the world-famous Charles Lindbergh visited the Yakima Valley as part of a nationwide fund-raising tour.

Left: Horse-drawn wagon on the John W. Monroe orchard in Grandview, circa 1905. *Bleyhl Community Library, Grandview*

Right: Northern Pacific Depot, North Yakima, circa 1910. The fourth Northern Pacific Railroad Depot. Built 1909 and opened May 1910. Located on Front Street. *Yakima Valley Museum*

Above: Northern Pacific Depot and park, North Yakima, early 1900s. A 900 foot cement platform and park with fountains was constructed for the new depot. To the left you can see the Switzer Opera House. *Yakima Valley Museum*

Right: Train wreck at Selah Creek, January 12, 1902. *Yakima Valley Museum*

Below: Mule pack train on Yakima Avenue, North Yakima, 1905. *Yakima Valley Museum*

Above: Street workers grading Ninth and Yakima avenues, North Yakima, early 1900s. *Yakima Valley Museum*

Left: Passenger train at the Yakima Depot, 1908. In the background is the third North Yakima Northern Pacific Depot, constructed in 1898. A section of it was moved north to Cherry Avenue where it was used as part of a duplex. In the foreground of this picture are crossing frogs laid over the railroad tracks by Northern Pacific and paid for by the Yakima Valley Transportation Company. *Yakima Valley Museum*

Above: Street car No. 8 (Maple Street) and the Fruitvale car converge near Geoff's Market, North Yakima, early 1900s. *Yakima Valley Museum*

Left: Yakima Valley Transportation Company Maple Street trolley, an original Danville type streetcar, North Yakima, circa 1910. Notice the advertisement for the Yakima Theatre on the cow catcher, "Lew Dockstader 7 Big Reels any seat 10 cents." *Yakima Valley Museum*

Below Left: A row of pack horses in Yakima City, circa 1900. *Yakima Valley Museum, George Martin collection*

Below Right: Lyman Bunting is the passenger in this 1910 photo taken in North Yakima. Note steering wheel on right side. *Rod MacKintosh*

Above: Laying trolley track down Yakima Avenue at the corner of Yakima Avenue and Front Street, North Yakima, circa 1907. *Yakima Valley Museum*

Left: A buggy ride down Yakima Avenue, North Yakima, circa 1915. *R. MacKintosh*

Right: A 1914 Dodge received by Railroad Express from Detroit. *Yakima Valley Museum*

Below: Yakima Valley Transportation Co. construction train on Yakima Avenue in North Yakima during the summer of 1908. This 0-4-0 steam locomotive was purchased second hand. This view is looking east from the intersection of First Street. Mr. Keyezers is the engineer. *Yakima Valley Museum*

Above: A photographer, visiting homes with a goat and cart, captures a member of the Hess family, North Yakima, circa 1910. *Elizabeth Irons*

Above, left: Motorman Mark S. Graves and conductor Pat Potter in front of their street car, Fourth Street North, North Yakima, circa 1918. Notice the banner on the cow catcher announcing the football game at Sumach Park. *Yakima Valley Museum*

Left: A Union Pacific Railroad survey crew take a rest break, circa 1917. *Yakima Valley Museum*

Above: Mrs. Margaret Porter purchased the first ticket to Yakima on Tex Rankin's flight service, spring 1928. The airplane duplicated Charles Lindbergh's and was flown by Frank Vanderline. People are identified, from left: ___ ___,City Commissioner Bigelow, Mrs. Porter, County Commissioner Frank Shull and Frank Vanderline. *Yakima Valley Museum*

Left: Campbell Construction Company road crew based out of Sunnyside, working on a rock crusher near Mabton, circa 1922. *Yakima Valley Museum*

Below: A group of people posing with a bi-wing aircraft at the Yakima Airport, circa 1925. *Yakima Valley Regional Library*

Above: Aviator Charles Lindbergh flew over the Central Washington State Fairgrounds, then flew on to Seattle as a benefit for the United States mail service, circa 1928. *R. MacKintosh*

Above Right: First passenger flying service in and out of Yakima, 1932. *Yakima Valley Museum*

Right: A row of cross-state buses lined up at the Yakima Train Station in the 1930s. *Yakima Valley Museum*

Below Right: Mr. Marble (left) and Ed Riley are the first passengers to take a ride from the Yakima County Airport, June 1928. *Yakima Valley Regional Library*

Below: Horse-drawn wagon near Prosser dam, circa 1910. Notice the mill in the left of the photo. *Yakima Valley Museum*

CHAPTER THREE

The Water Flows

The semi-arid brush land of the Yakima Valley provided ample grazing for the herds of cattle and bands of sheep that made up the area's earliest agriculture. But for the diversity of crops that was to become the trademark of the Yakima Valley, they needed water — and lots of it.

As Ka-mi-akin of the Yakamas can claim credit for the first commercial cattle operation, he is also credited, along with the Catholic priests, with the first ditch irrigation — a simple system to bring water to the gardens at the Ahtanum Mission in 1849.

That was followed by hand-dug irrigation ditches and hand-built flumes throughout the Valley, diverting water from every river, creek and stream for the increasingly diverse crops that grew in the region's fertile soil. An estimated three dozen ditch companies began work throughout the Valley in the 1880s and 1890s.

The U.S. Reclamation Act of 1902 completed the work started by the ditch companies. The federal government built a series of five reservoirs — Bumping, Kachess, Keechelus, Rimrock and Cle Elum — on the east flank of the Cascade Mountains in fewer than 25 years. Today, the Yakima Valley remains dependent on the dams and irrigation systems of the last century.

Left: American Indians fish at Prosser dam, early 1900. Taylor mill is seen on the other side of the river. *Yakima Valley Museum*

Right: Crew constructing the canal intake of the Naches-Selah Canal, 1907. *Yakima Valley Museum*

Above: Rock crusher at work during the construction of the Congdon Ditch near Painted Rocks, 1893. *Yakima Valley Museum*

Right: Work crew on the Bumping Lake project, circa 1910. *Yakima Valley Museum*

Far Right: Placing open canal concrete C-shaped lining sections during construction work on the Tieton Irrigation system, July 1909. *Yakima Valley Museum*

Above: Irrigation project, Lake Kachess, 1910.
Yakima Valley Museum

Left: Close-up of double syphon on the Congdon Ditch at Painted Rocks, circa 1910.
Yakima Valley Museum

Right: Dam construction at Lake Kachess, circa 1910.
Yakima Valley Museum

The staff of Yakima Regional Medical and Cardiac Center and Toppenish Community Hospital are proud to continue a 113-year legacy of medical expertise in Central Washington. Today, our hospitals are building on that tradition by providing compassionate, quality care with the most advanced medical technology available, including open heart surgery, efficient and expert emergency care, neurosurgery, and rehabilitation.

Thank you for putting your trust in Yakima Regional and Toppenish Community Hospital!

36.718622.YVM.F

Above: Method of hauling the concrete lining C-shaped sections during the Tieton Irrigation project construction, circa 1911. *Yakima Valley Museum*

Left: Loading 8-inch reinforced cement pipe at Camp 12, Wide Hollow, during the Tieton Irrigation Project construction, June 1911. *Yakima Valley Museum*

Below: Construction work continues on the Tieton Irrigation project, circa 1911. *Yakima Valley Museum*

Left: Laying and joining 10-inch concrete pipe during the Tieton Irrigation Project construction, circa 1911. *Yakima Valley Museum*

Above and Below: Construction of the Rimrock Dam on the Tieton River, circa 1920. *Yakima Valley Museum*

Above and Below: Rimrock Dam construction in the early 1920s. Dam dedicated July 1925. *Yakima Valley Museum*

Right: General view of the gate tower at Rimrock Dam, July 8, 1916. *Yakima Valley Museum*

CHAPTER FOUR

WORKING THE LAND

In 1849, Ka-mi-akin of the Yakamas traveled to Fort Vancouver and traded horses to the Hudson Bay Company for some black Spanish cattle. That was the first recorded venture into what would in a very few years become the economic backbone of the Yakima Valley: agriculture.

Within 20 years, F. Mortimer Thorp established the first real cattle ranch in Moxee. And the crops to feed the growing herds of cattle — and, by 1861, sheep — were planted throughout the Valley.

French settlers in the Moxee area had impressive hop farms as early as 1890, and by the early 1900s the Yakima Valley's diverse crops were already being carried by rail throughout the nation. Peaches were harvested commercially by 1900, with apples, pears, plums and prunes all added within a decade.

With the increasing production came the addition of packing houses clustered near the rail depot along Yakima's Front and First streets.

In 1888, the North Yakima rail depot showed receipts of $168,000 for rail shipments of the Valley's agriculture — cattle, sheep, hay, vegetables, potatoes, melons, wool and even leaf tobacco.

Left: Stacking hay on the ranch of James Gleed, 1897, just west of North Yakima at a place where the settlement of Gleed was named for him. *Yakima Valley Museum*

Right: Hop pickers pose for the photo on the Jim Harvey ranch in Wide Hollow, circa 1890. *Yakima Valley Museum*

Above: Threshing machine and crew of W.H. Minner near Wiley City-Minner ranch, 1881. His son, J.E. (Dude) Minner is driving. *Yakima Valley Museum*

Right: View of George Hull's ranch, Selah Valley, 1890. *Yakima Valley Museum*

Below: Walter White's hop kiln at Gleed, 1894. *Yakima Valley Museum*

Left: H.D. Winchester's kiln built by C. Schwemsen, 1894. *Yakima Valley Museum*

Right: Hop picking at the John Monder Ranch in the Ahtanum, 1895. *Yakima Valley Museum*

Below: Grain harvesting crew, circa 1895. *Yakima Valley Museum*

Left: T.H. Smith's sheep camp, Moxee, east of North Yakima, 1898. *Yakima Valley Museum*

Right: Haying in the Nile Valley, circa 1910. *Yakima Valley Museum*

Below: Home, orchard and garden of E.L. Blaine, in Grandview, circa 1910. *Yakima Valley Museum*

Right: Packing peaches at J. Van Payton Ranch, circa 1900. *Yakima Valley Museum*

Below Right: Hop pickers in the Yakima Valley, early 1900s. Some are identified as Vern Harrison, Harland Pierce, Mrs. George, Vida Cavlin, Lottie George, Hazel Cavlin. *Yakima Valley Museum*

Below: Hop pickers decorate themselves with strings of hops around their necks and hats, early 1900s. *Yakima Valley Museum*

Above: Threshing crew in the Prosser area, circa 1907.
Yakima Valley Museum

Right: Haying in Cowiche, 1906. Left to right: Mr. And Mrs. Danker, Annie, Henry, Katie, Emma, Clarence Hobbs. Others identified as E.A.Van Epps, Earl Hartwell and Mike Schuler. *Yakima Valley Museum*

Below Tying grapes for planting in the Yakima Valley, 1908.
Yakima Valley Museum

Above: A horse drawn wagon loaded with apples in front of A.E. Larson's house on Yakima Avenue, North Yakima, circa 1909. *Yakima Valley Museum*

Above Left: Sorting apples on the H.M. Gilbert orchard, November 6, 1909. *Yakima Valley Museum*

Middle Left: Cantaloupes were harvested on this tract of land in Zillah, circa 1910. 150 crates per acre were harvested and then sold at an average price of $2 per crate. Such a practice of planting crops in new orchards was common until the trees began to produce saleable fruit. *Yakima Valley Museum*

Below Left: Lee Chamberlain's haying crew in the Prosser area, circa 1907. *Yakima Valley Museum*

Below: Workers packing apples in orchard, circa 1910. *Yakima Valley Museum*

Above: Apple pickers take a break to have their photo taken, circa 1910.
Yakima Valley Museum

Right: Packing apples at the outdoor packing yard on the L.B. Kinyon ranch, North Yakima, circa 1910. *Yakima Valley Museum*

Below Right: Shipping fruit at the J.M. Perry packing and shipping house. Perry had the first ice plant in North Yakima, 1910. *Yakima Valley Museum*

Below: Milking cows on a ranch in the Yakima Valley, circa 1910.
Yakima Valley Museum

Above: A Yakima Valley beekeeper, circa 1910.

Yakima Valley Museum

Above Left: Peach packing crew on the Huxtable Ranch located at Barge and 24th Avenue, circa 1910.

Yakima Valley Museum

Left: Packing peaches at the Thompson Fruit Company, North Yakima, circa 1912. Note overseer standing on the left side.

Yakima Valley Museum

Above: American Indian hop-pickers camp, 1916. *Yakima Valley Museum*

Left: Mrs. Hutchings (Mrs. Frank Lanterman's mother), far left, with her family picking hops. Mrs. Lanterman, third from right, came to visit her family. The family lived in a tent during the hop season, 1913. *Jack Whitnall Collection, Frank Lanterman, photographer*

Below: Hop pickers at the kiln at Morrier's hop ranch, Moxee, 1913. The Morrier ranch is still producing hops. *Yakima Valley Museum*

Above: Workers at a fruit packing warehouse in Yakima pose for a photo on the loading dock, circa 1920. *Yakima Valley Museum*

Right: Construction at the Utah-Idaho Sugar Refinery, Sunnyside, June 3, 1919. *Yakima Valley Museum*

Below: Hecox Processing Company plant at North First Avenue, Yakima, 1920. *Joseph Hecox*

Below Left: Crew working at a tree nursery with eight-mule team in Toppenish, circa 1923. *Yakima Valley Museum*

Above: Northwest Fruit Company warehouse in Gleed, early 1920s. *Yakima Valley Museum*

Opposite page: Picking Spitzenberg apples on the E.G. Van Brundt ranch, 1918. *Yakima Valley Museum*

Left top: A few of the 80 employees at the Yakima warehouse of the Big Y showing the two sizing machines, and the packing crew with part of their day's pack on the roller conveyors waiting for the lidder to nail on the tops and shoot the packed boxes down to the cold storage rooms. Every packer put a ticket, bearing her number on the top of the fruit, the lidder removed the tickets and placed them in piles, and the packers' wages, 5 cents a box, were paid on the basis of the tickets turned in, circa 1923. *Yakima Valley Museum*

Left bottom: The women in the foreground were sorters – looking over every apple as it passed over the belts, to see whether it was worthy to be packed under the Big Y label. After these women sorted for grade, the sizing machine droped them according to size into bins from which the packers wrapped them and arranged them in the boxes – and a good packer would have packed nearly a box of them while you are reading this. This photo is in the packing room of the Big Y cold storage plant at Sawyer, circa 1923. *Yakima Valley Museum*

Above: An early local promoter stated the following about the Yakima Valley: "Noted all over the world for its magnificent fruit and well kept orchards, the Yakima Valley represents the highest point reached in intensive horticulture as well as in methods of caring for fruit and preparing it for market. The quality of its fruit is due partly to the scientific methods used in raising it, but also to the rich volcanic ash soil and the distinctive climate of the valley." This view is from Lookout Mountain and overlooks the city of Yakima, circa 1920. *Yakima Valley Museum*

Left: Beekeepers S. King Clover and his brother Clarence Clover, 7951 Emerald Road, Sunnyside, 1920. *Norma Friend*

Below: The Big Y warehouse at Grandview, which was the second largest fruit shipping point in the Yakima Valley in about 1920 and needed a crew of 50 employees to receive, receipt for, truck in, pack and otherwise prepare for market the immense tonnage of apples grown in this district. As in many others of the 13 Big Y plants, the women outnumbered the men, as all sorters and nearly all packers were women. The men did the trucking, dumping, piling and other heavy work, circa 1923. *Yakima Valley Museum*

Above: Washington State Woolgrowers pose in front of Hotel Commercial in Yakima, January 26, 1926. *Yakima Valley Museum*

Left: Scene at Sawyer cold storage plant of the Big Y during apple harvest, showing some of the elevators that lift the boxes from the ranchers' wagons directly to the storage rooms. During the 1923 pear harvest more than 11,000 boxes of pears were received and lifted to the cold rooms in one day. *Yakima Valley Museum*

Below: Winter time at McGregor's sheep ranch in the Prosser area, 1920s. *Yakima Valley Museum*

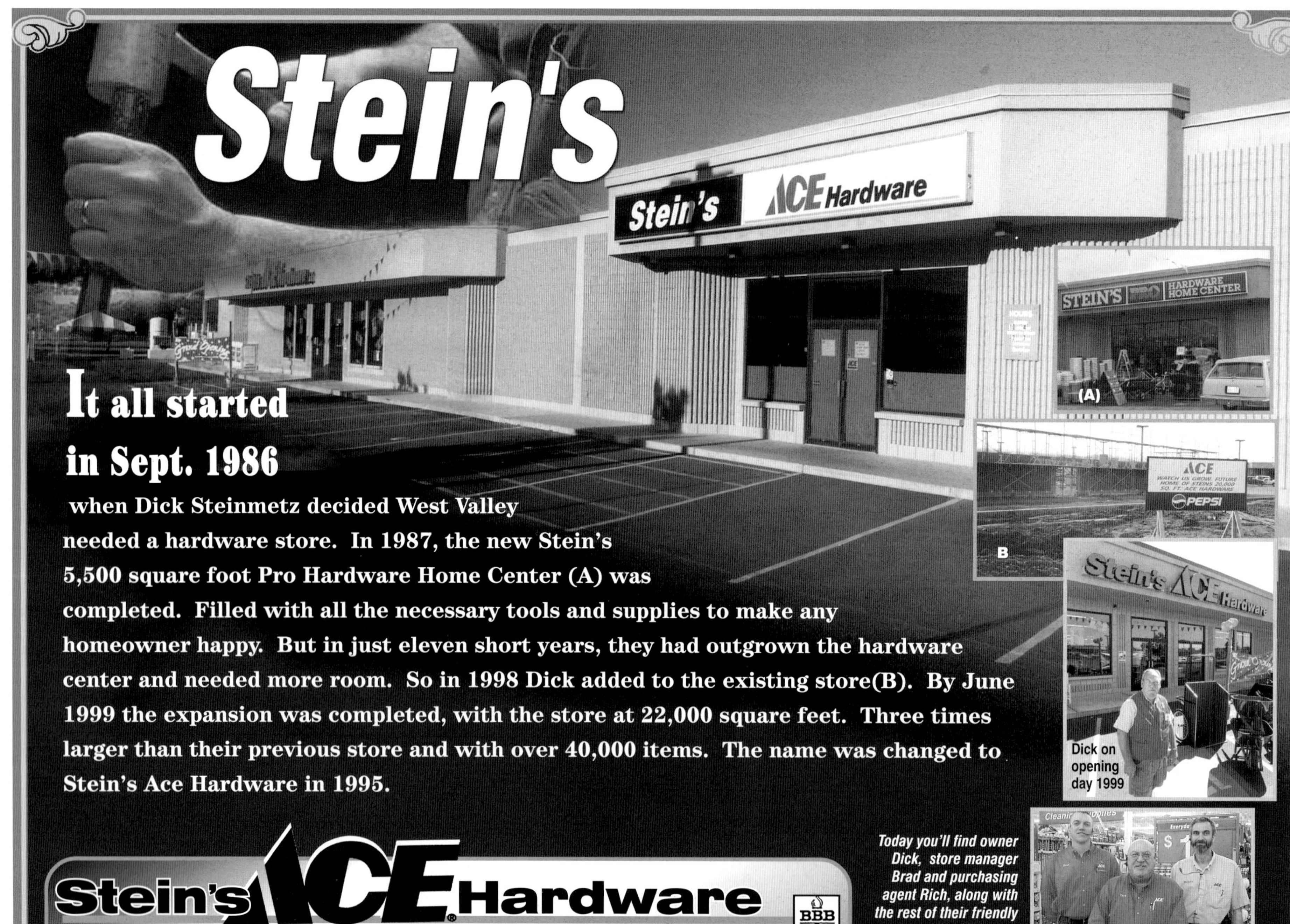
Stein's
Stein's
ACE Hardware
STEIN'S
HARDWARE HOME CENTER
(A)
ACE
WATCH US GROW. FUTURE HOME OF STEINS 20,000 SQ. FT. ACE HARDWARE
PEPSI
B
Stein's ACE Hardware
It all started in Sept. 1986
when Dick Steinmetz decided West Valley needed a hardware store. In 1987, the new Stein's 5,500 square foot Pro Hardware Home Center (A) was completed. Filled with all the necessary tools and supplies to make any homeowner happy. But in just eleven short years, they had outgrown the hardware center and needed more room. So in 1998 Dick added to the existing store(B). By June 1999 the expansion was completed, with the store at 22,000 square feet. Three times larger than their previous store and with over 40,000 items. The name was changed to Stein's Ace Hardware in 1995.
Dick on opening day 1999
Stein's ACE Hardware
M-F 7AM-7PM • SAT. 8AM-6PM
SUN 9AM-4PM
965-2622 • 7200 W. NOB HILL BLVD.
...in the Meadowbrook Shopping Center
BBB
Today you'll find owner Dick, store manager Brad and purchasing agent Rich, along with the rest of their friendly staff, ready to help you with all your residential and commercial needs.
Brad, Dick and Rich

Above Left: Pouring in the apples that had been precooked for the oversized apple pie promotion, "When Yakima Baked the Big Apple Pie," in 1927. *Yakima Valley Museum*

Above Right: An oversized apple pie was prepared in 1927 as a promotion in Yakima, "When Yakima Baked the Big Apple Pie." A thousand people had a slice of this 18 foot pie. *Yakima Valley Museum*

Left: Yakima Fruit Growers Association delivery truck and trailer, Yakima, circa 1929. *Yakima Valley Museum*

Below: Libby, McNeill & Libby employees gather for a photograph in front of their plant, Yakima, circa 1925. *Yakima Valley Museum*

Above: Packing Yakima Valley apples, circa 1935. Man in center is John Sak. *Yakima Valley Museum*

Above Right: Sorting apples in the Yakima Valley, 1930s. *Yakima Valley Museum*

Right: Sacks of onions on a farm near Toppenish, 1930s. *Yakima Valley Museum*

Above: Turkey caretaker Ned Barrett on the Broadway turkey farm, Yakima, 1936. *Yakima Valley Museum*

Right: Robert Cowin strapping Golden Delicious apples for Amelia Earhart before her ill-fated flight, 1937. *Douglas E. Cowin*

Below: Fruit packing district, Selah, circa 1940s. *Yakima Valley Museum*

BARNES-WOODIN CO.
Bush & Lane Piano
MILLINER

CHAPTER FIVE

COMMERCE THRIVES

The business of the Yakima Valley was agriculture, but it attracted a wide range of commerce to support it. And since the earliest days, Yakima City had been a hub for saloons, hotels and dry goods stores. In 1870, it was named county seat. In 1883, the city that would eventually be known as Union Gap was incorporated. (Ellensburg was incorporated the same year.)

The arrival of Northern Pacific Railway and the four-mile move to North Yakima in 1885 marked the beginning of a commercial boom for the fledgling city.

By the end of 1885, the new commercial hub boasted 15 lawyers, three doctors and one dentist, four hotels, four general stores, four livery stables, a telegraph office, a shop shoe, two meat markets, a brick yard, two tailors, five real estate agents, an ice cream parlor, seven laundries, two agricultural warehouses, three weekly newspapers, five restaurants, 15 saloons and a "$4,500 railroad depot."

While the scale was smaller and the speed slower, numerous other towns in the Valley also incorporated within the next couple of decades: Toppenish in 1887, Prosser in 1899, Cle Elum and Sunnyside in 1902, Mabton in 1905, Wapato in 1908 and Grandview and Granger in 1909.

Left: Crowd lines up for a special sale outside Barnes-Woodin Company in North Yakima, circa 1912. *Yakima Valley Museum*

Right: Weed and Rowe Hardware Store, located at the corner of Yakima Avenue and First Street, circa 1896. This business later became Yakima Hardware. This building was moved up from Yakima City in 1885. *Yakima Valley Museum*

Above: Yakima National Bank, 102 East Yakima Avenue, North Yakima, 1890. Pictured, left to right, George Donald, president; Leonard Thorp, vice-president; John D. Cornett, cashier; Frank Bartholet, assistant. *Yakima Valley Museum*

Above Left: Hotel Yakima on the corner of Third Street and Yakima Avenue, North Yakima, circa 1890. Note street condition. *Yakima Valley Museum*

Below Left: Exterior view of Guilland House in Yakima City, circa 1884. *Yakima Valley Museum*

Below: Interior of Allen & Chapman's Drug Store, North Yakima, 1890. *Yakima Valley Museum*

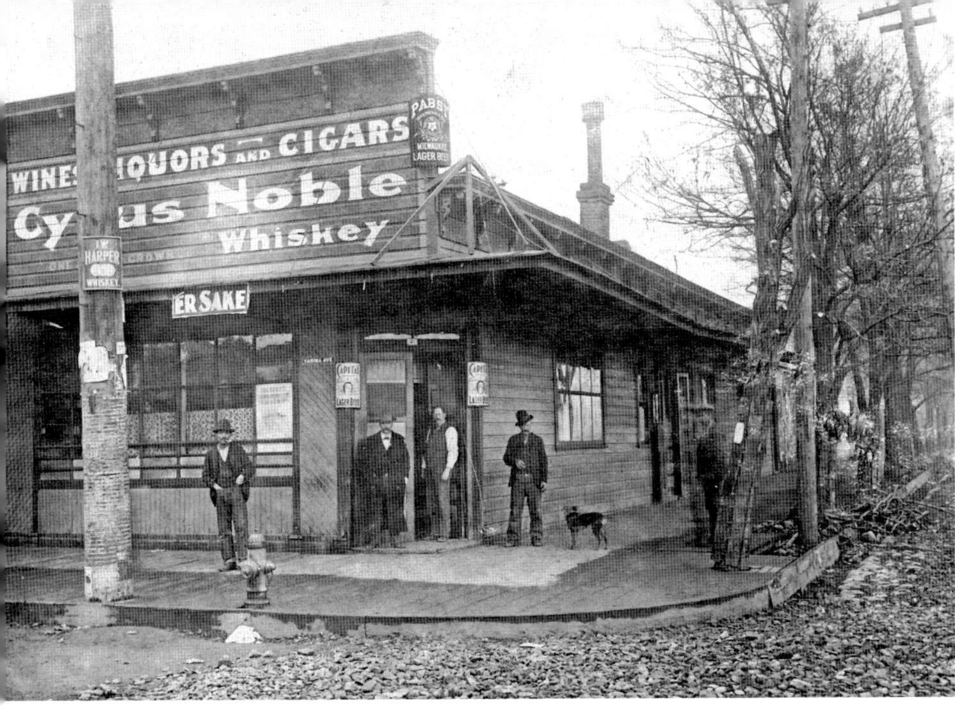

Above: Stage arriving from the train station to pick up passengers at Hotel Bartholet on North First Street, North Yakima, 1890. *Yakima Valley Museum*

Above Left: Exterior view of the Cyrus Noble saloon located on the corner of Front Street and Yakima Avenue, North Yakima, circa 1890. *Yakima Valley Museum*

Left: Barber shop and ice cream parlor on Yakima Avenue between Front and First streets in Yakima, circa 1900. *Yakima Valley Museum*

Below: Fashion Stables and carriage room, Fourth Street and Yakima Avenue, late 1800s. The owner was Fred J.C. Brooker. *Yakima Valley Museum*

Above: Interior of blacksmith shop on North Front Street, North Yakima, circa 1900. *Yakima Valley Museum*

Above Right: Fred Benoit's Meat Market in North Yakima at the corner of Yakima and First, early 1900s. The market was located where Wells Fargo Bank is today. *Frank Benoit*

Right: Chicago dry goods store 8-10 South Second Street, Yakima, circa 1899. It burned in early 1900. *Yakima Valley Museum*

Below: A. H. Wilgus, horseshoer, located on Front Street, Yakima, circa 1900. *Yakima Valley Museum*

Above: Yakima National Bank, 102 East Yakima Avenue, North Yakima, circa 1903. This was the first National Bank in the state. *Yakima Valley Museum*

Right: Coffin Bros. Department store, Third and Yakima avenues, North Yakima, early 1900s. *Yakima Valley Museum*

Right Below: Ditter Brothers store, 109-111 East Yakima Avenue, North Yakima, circa 1904. Ditter Brothers moved their business from Yakima City to North Yakima in 1885. *Christine Corbett Conklin*

Below: A.E. Larson's Theatre located on North Second and A streets, circa 1900. Sign for current feature at the theatre says, "Why Women Sin." The clocks seen in this photo were placed in the new county courthouse when the theatre was torn down. *Yakima Valley Museum*

Above: Grandview livery stable. Marvin Martin proprietor 1910. *Bleyhl Community Library, Grandview*

Right: Hotel Toppenish shortly after it opened in 1907. *Yakima Valley Museum*

Below: Yakima Valley Steam & Laundry, North Yakima, May 19, 1908. *Yakima Valley Museum*

Above: Palace Hotel, Prosser, circa 1910. *Yakima Valley Museum*

Left: Employees of the Cascade Lumber Company, Yakima, 1910. *Elizabeth Irons*

Below Left: Henry B. Scudder, left, sitting, Marshall Scudder, sitting center, circa 1910. Business is in the Schreiner Building on Second Street, North Yakima. *Yakima Valley Museum*

Below: Front view of Bartley's Drug Store in Zillah, circa 1908. Notice the goats are pulling a wagon with toasted corn flakes. *Yakima Valley Museum*

Above: Interior view of Janeck Drug Store at 109 East Yakima Avenue, North Yakima, circa 1910. *Yakima Valley Museum*

Above Right: H. M. Gilbert Real Estate office in Toppenish, circa 1910. *Yakima Valley Museum*

Right: A two-horse commercial dray hauling bottled water parks in front of Miller Building on Yakima Avenue, North Yakima, circa 1910. *Yakima Valley Museum*

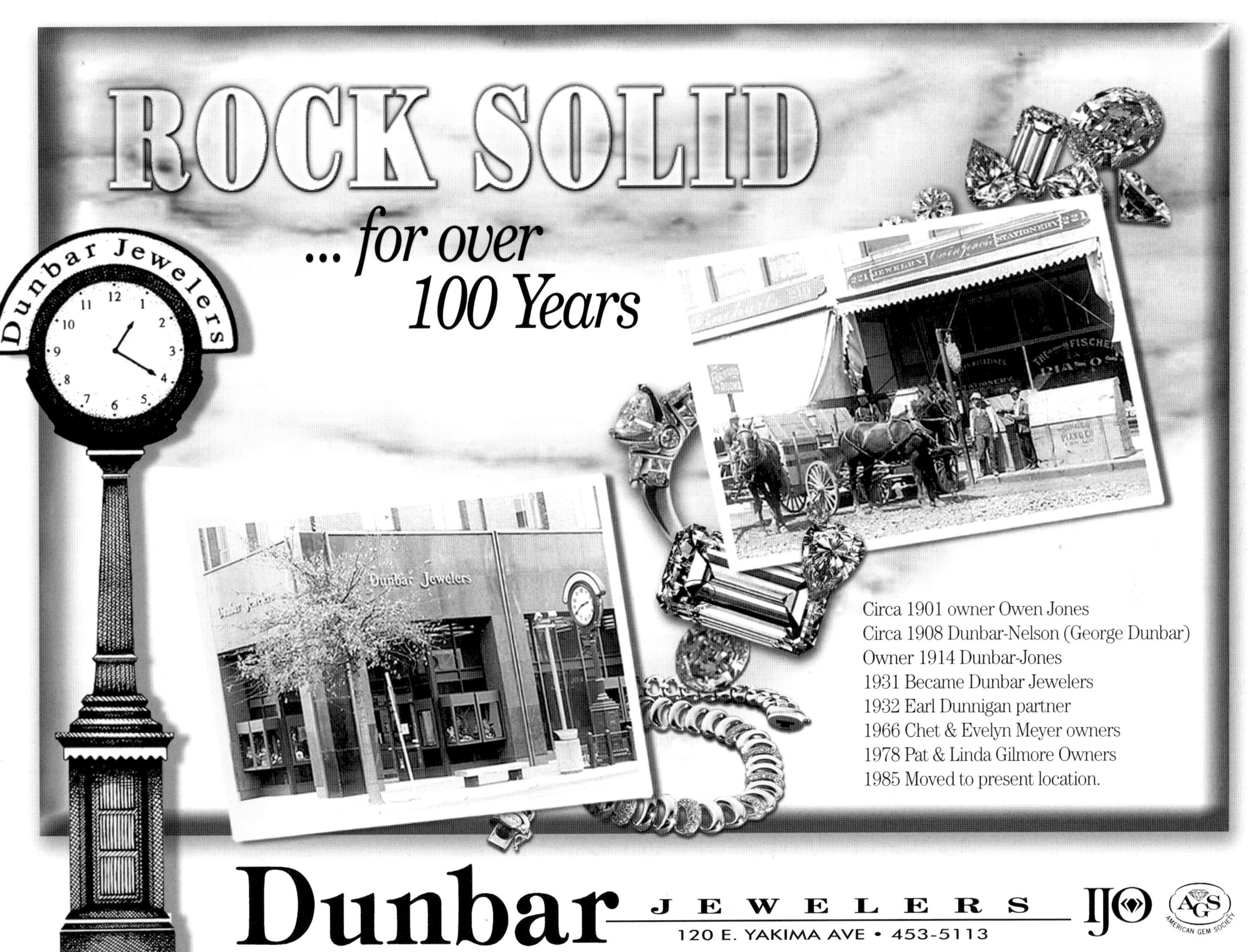
ROCK SOLID
...for over 100 Years
Dunbar Jewelers
Dunbar Jewelers
Circa 1901 owner Owen Jones
Circa 1908 Dunbar-Nelson (George Dunbar)
Owner 1914 Dunbar-Jones
1931 Became Dunbar Jewelers
1932 Earl Dunnigan partner
1966 Chet & Evelyn Meyer owners
1978 Pat & Linda Gilmore Owners
1985 Moved to present location.
Dunbar JEWELERS
120 E. YAKIMA AVE • 453-5113
IJO
AGS
AMERICAN GEM SOCIETY
46.719236.yvm.F

Above: Interior of the First National Bank at 124 East Yakima Avenue, North Yakima, circa 1910. *Yakima Valley Museum*

Above Right: American Indian women displaying their wares for sale, circa 1910. *Yakima Valley Museum*

Right: Commercial Hotel and the Wilson Building located on Third and Yakima avenues, North Yakima, circa 1912. John Jacob Miller built the Commercial Hotel in 1911. George Wilson built the Wilson Building in 1902. Both buildings are still standing today. *Yakima Valley Museum*

Left: Bell-Wyman Company at Front and A streets, Yakima, circa 1915. *Marily K. Roll*

Below Left: Interior view of the Sunset Market owned by James Frances, North Yakima, circa 1914.

Yakima Valley Museum

Below: H.G. Rideout, Richey & Gilbert's Fruit Company treasurer, April 4, 1918.

Yakima Valley Museum

Right: Empire building on Second Street, circa 1920. It was remodeled in 1931 and renamed the Yakima Theatre. *Yakima Valley Museum*

Below: Employees of the W.W. Sheane Auto Company, 1920. Left to right, lower row: Wallace Richardson, unidentified, Tim Flannigan, Andy Bogard, unidentified, Geo. Barton, Earl Clevenger, Dean Shimpton, unidentified, Joe Yolo, A. Walker, Russel Rowan, Wm. Beaupra, Harry Thomas, unidentified, unidentified, ____Henderson, Harry Koser, unidentified, unidentified, Virgil Williams, unidentified, Wm. Smith, Emory Hale, unidentified, D.G. Parriott, ____Spitzmesser, unidentified, Ward Dean. Upper row: Charley Cripps, unidentified, Bob Steindorf, Richard Korth, Rowland Brown, unidentified, Leonard Brown, unidentified. *Yakima Valley Museum*

Above: Interior of a local harness shop, North Yakima, circa 1900. *Yakima Valley Museum*

Above Left: Interior of Redlinger & Hale City Markets, Sunnyside, circa 1920. *Yakima Valley Museum*

Left: Ditter Brothers store display windows, 109-111 East Yakima Avenue in downtown Yakima, circa 1920. *Christine Corbett Conklin*

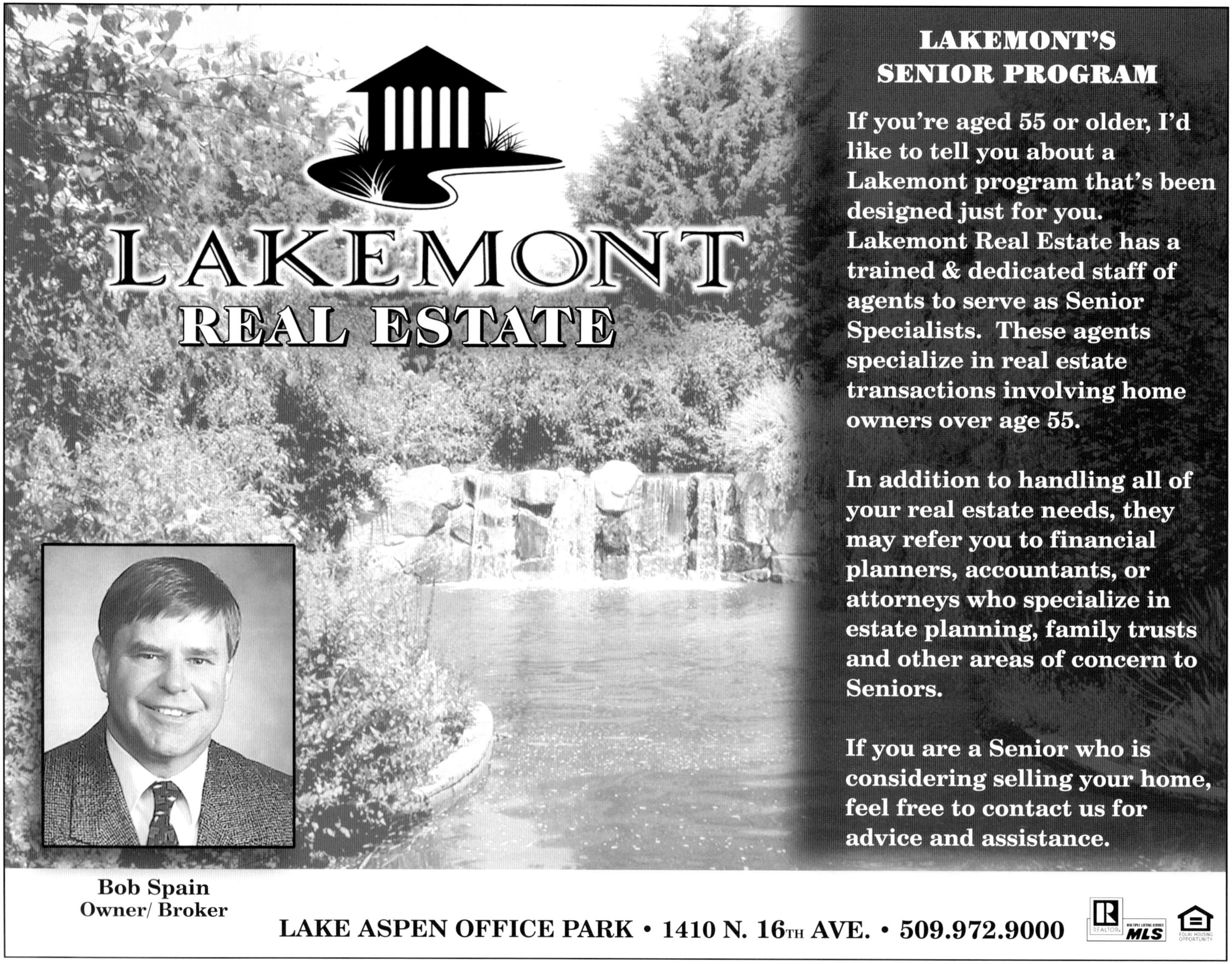
LAKEMONT
REAL ESTATE
LAKEMONT'S
SENIOR PROGRAM
If you're aged 55 or older, I'd like to tell you about a Lakemont program that's been designed just for you. Lakemont Real Estate has a trained & dedicated staff of agents to serve as Senior Specialists. These agents specialize in real estate transactions involving home owners over age 55.
In addition to handling all of your real estate needs, they may refer you to financial planners, accountants, or attorneys who specialize in estate planning, family trusts and other areas of concern to Seniors.
If you are a Senior who is considering selling your home, feel free to contact us for advice and assistance.
Bob Spain
Owner/ Broker
LAKE ASPEN OFFICE PARK • 1410 N. 16TH AVE. • 509.972.9000
REALTOR
MLS
EQUAL HOUSING OPPORTUNITY

Left: Street view of Talcott's Music Store with delivery vehicle in foreground, Yakima, circa 1925. *Yakima Valley Museum*

Right: A crowd shows up for the going out of business sale at Dean Clothing Company, located at 111 East Yakima Avenue, Yakima, circa 1922. Yakima Valley Bank is at right. *Yakima Valley Museum*

Below: Highway Service Station, circa 1921. *Yakima Valley Museum*

Right: Delivery truck and car in front of Dobson Motor Company at 204 North First, Yakima, circa 1926. Notice the advertisements that say: "Red Crown Gasoline - 30 Miles to the Gallon. $785.00 for Car." *Yakima Valley Museum*

Below: Crowd advertises a Maytag aluminum washer promotion in front of Skagg's Safeway store and W.H.M. Clinton produce dealer, circa 1927. *Yakima Valley Museum*

Above: The first Model A Ford sold in Sunnyside to Mark Austin by Roscoe Sheller of Sheller Motor Company, the first Ford agent in the Valley, circa 1920s. *Yakima Valley Museum*

Above: Peerless Laundry, First and B streets, Yakima, 1924. *Yakima Valley Museum*

Right: Ditter Bros., 109-11 East Yakima Avenue, spring style show, Yakima, March 22, 1925. *Yakima Valley Museum*

Below: Night view of Barnes-Woodin Department Store at Third and Yakima Avenue, Yakima, decorated for Christmas in the 1920s. The International Order Of Odd Fellows met upstairs. *Yakima Valley Museum*

Left: Weber Chevrolet, located on the corner of Third Street and Chestnut Avenue, Yakima, operated by John H. Weber, circa 1940. *Yakima Valley Museum*

Right: Wikstrom Motors, Inc. at 109-111 S. Third Street, Yakima, owned by William Wikstrom, circa 1937. The fire station tower can be seen in the background. *Yakima Valley Museum*

Above: The Sugar Bowl Bakery and Soda Fountain, Sunnyside, circa 1930. *Yakima Valley Museum*

Right: Workers in front of Barnes-Woodin, Third Street and Yakima Avenue, circa 1935. *Marily K. Roll*

Below: Capitol Theater, 195 Third Street, Yakima, 1930s. Notice the marquee is advertising a free pony and a Mickey Mouse matinee. Capitol Theatre was owned by Frederick Mercy who owned over 21 theaters at one time. *Yakima Valley Museum*

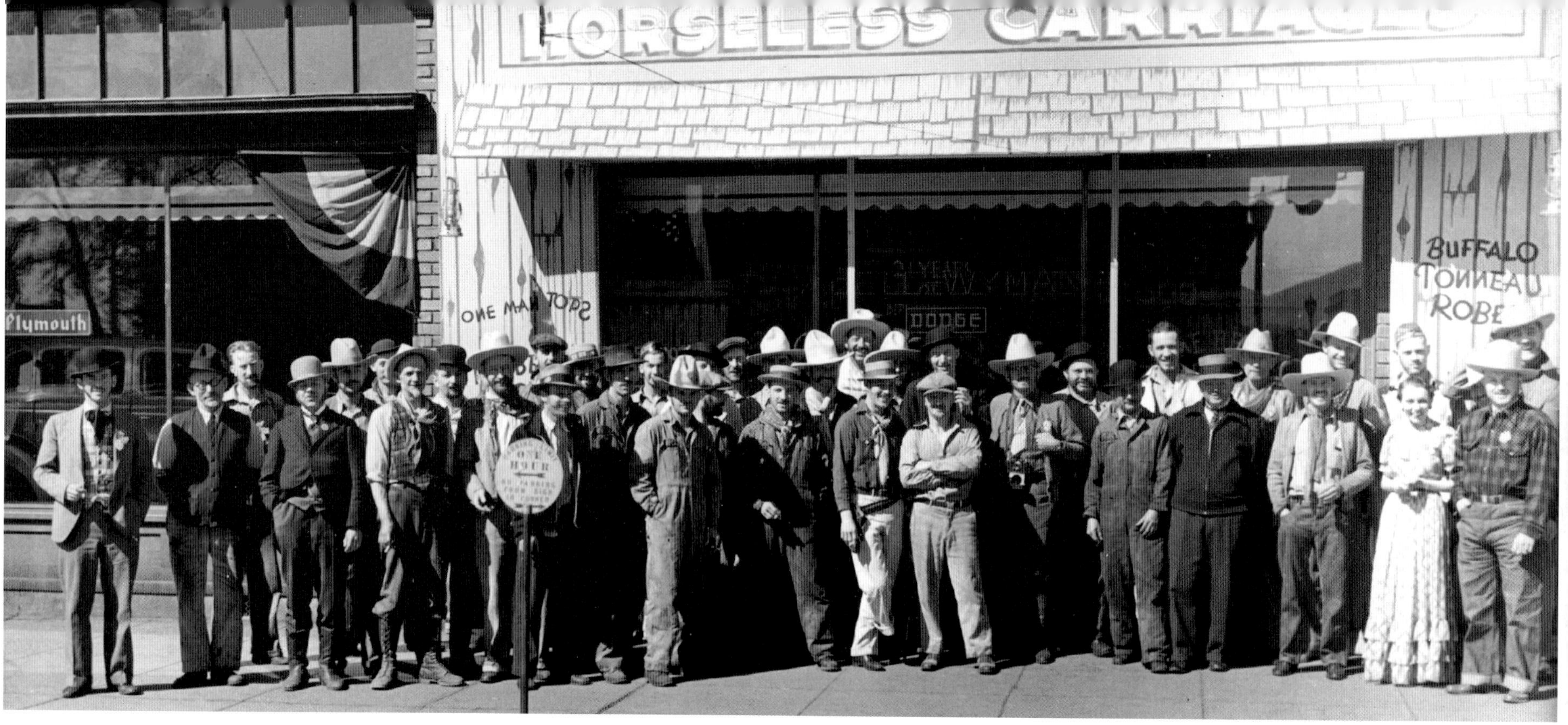

Above: Bell-Wyman Dodge employees dressed in "pioneer" clothes to celebrate Yakima's Golden Jubilee in front of the dealership at 102-114 S. First Street, Yakima, 1935. *Yakima Valley Museum*

Right: Interior of Weber's Chevrolet at the corner of Third Street and Chestnut Avenue, Yakima, 1930s. *Yakima Valley Museum*

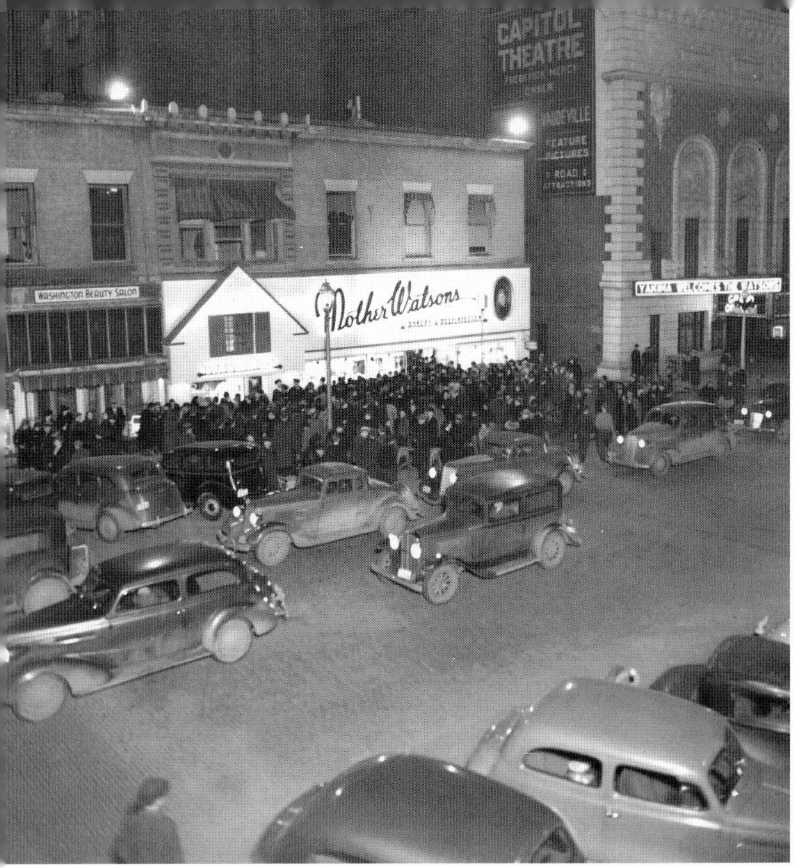

Above Left: Grand opening of Mother Watson's in Yakima, 1937. *Yakima Valley Museum*

Far Above: Row of Twin Bakery delivery trucks and drivers, 517 West Yakima Avenue, Yakima, 1930s. Notice the trucks are advertising soft bun bread. *Yakima Valley Museum*

Above: Kids line up outside Capitol Theater, Yakima in the 1930s. The boy on the pony is the winner of the contest advertised in the photo on page 78. *Yakima Valley Museum*

Left: Valley Auction House, 1930s. *Yakima Valley Museum*

AHTANUM ACADEMY

CHAPTER SIX

SCHOOLS & EDUCATION

There were 10 students in North Yakima's first high school graduating class on May 24, 1885. Today there are nearly 15,000 students in high schools throughout the Yakima Valley.

As the population of the Valley has grown, so have the opportunities for our children to receive a wide range of education.

Yakima's Central School, built in 1888 at 217 S. Second Street, was the Valley's first dedicated school building.

In Ellensburg, the Washington State Normal School — now known as Central Washington State University — opened to train teachers in 1891.

Yakima Valley Junior College opened in 1928, the third two-year institution in the state. Its first classes were held in the Columbia Grade School on North Fourth Avenue. Eventually renamed Yakima Valley Community College, it moved to its new campus at 16th Avenue and Nob Hill Boulevard in 1949.

The J.M. Perry Technical Institute opened in Yakima in 1941, realizing the dream of the late Yakima businessman whose plans for a vocational school were completed by his widow.

Heritage College — now University — was the latest addition to the educational landscape, opening in 1982 as a private independent college on Yakama Nation land near Toppenish.

Left: Woodcock Academy, a private school in Ahtanum, and the first high school in the Yakima Valley, 1892. The school was named for Fenn Woodcock and family. Fenn donated 60 acres of land for the school. The school burned to the ground in 2003. *Yakima Valley Museum*

Right: North Yakima's first school, Central School, 217 South Second Street, built in 1888, razed in 1924. The first graduation class in North Yakima was in 1894 with eight students. *Yakima Valley Museum*

Above: Interior view of classroom at Central School located at 217 South Second Street, circa 1900. Mrs. Ella Star was principal of high school classes at Central School. *Yakima Valley Museum*

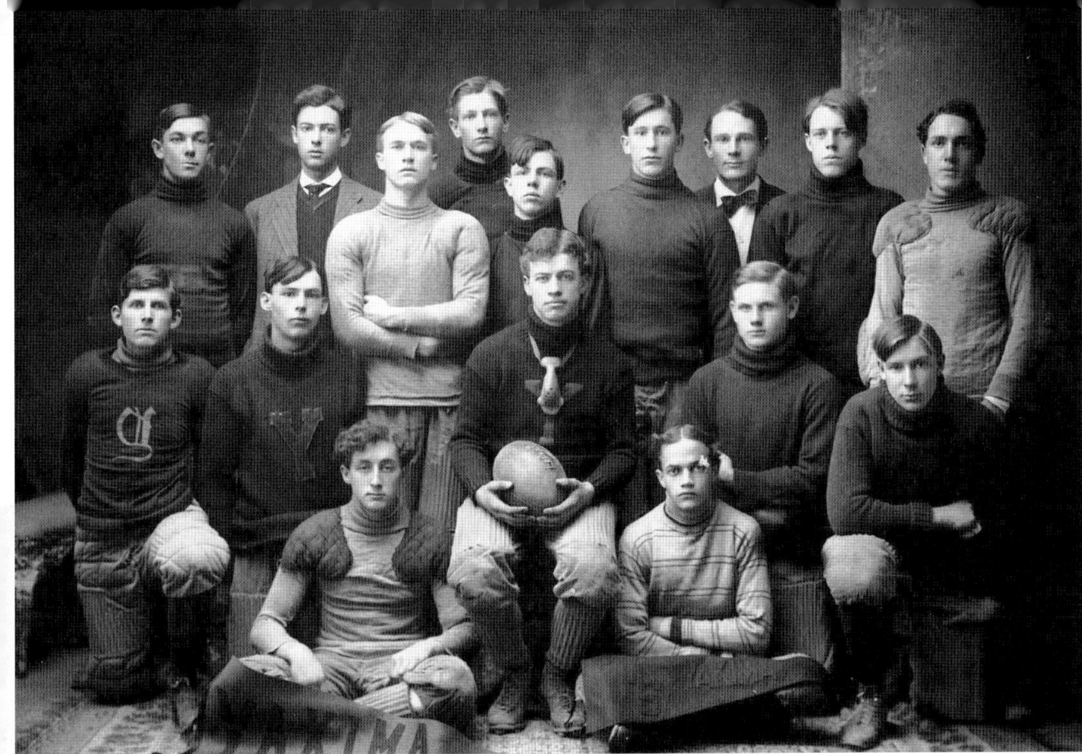

Above: Yakima High School football team, circa 1910. *Yakima Valley Museum*

Above Right: Riverside School building, Moxee, circa 1900. *Yakima Valley Museum*

Right: Columbia School located on North Fourth Avenue in North Yakima. This school was built in 1890 and used for high school and elementary classes. It is now the site of the YSD Administration offices. *Yakima Valley Museum*

Above: School kids in wagon with school building in background, Parker Heights, circa 1900. *Yakima Valley Museum*

Left: North Yakima High School track team, 1908. *Yakima Valley Museum*

Below: Barge School graduation class, North Yakima, 1909. *Yakima Valley Museum*

RE/MAX
Outstanding Agents
Outstanding Results
Jim Beckett
Broker-Owner,
CRB, CRS, ABR
Terry Harrington
Associate Broker-
Owner
Handling your Real Estate Matters with
care and pride is our goal.
RE/MAX
REAL ESTATE
37 HOUSE
853-3700
remax37house.com
EQUAL HOUSING
OPPORTUNITY

Above: Summitview elementary graduation class, North Yakima, 1909. *Yakima Valley Museum*

Left: North Yakima Central High School graduates, circa 1907. *Elizabeth Irons*

Below: North Yakima High School champion football team, 1909. *Yakima Valley Museum*

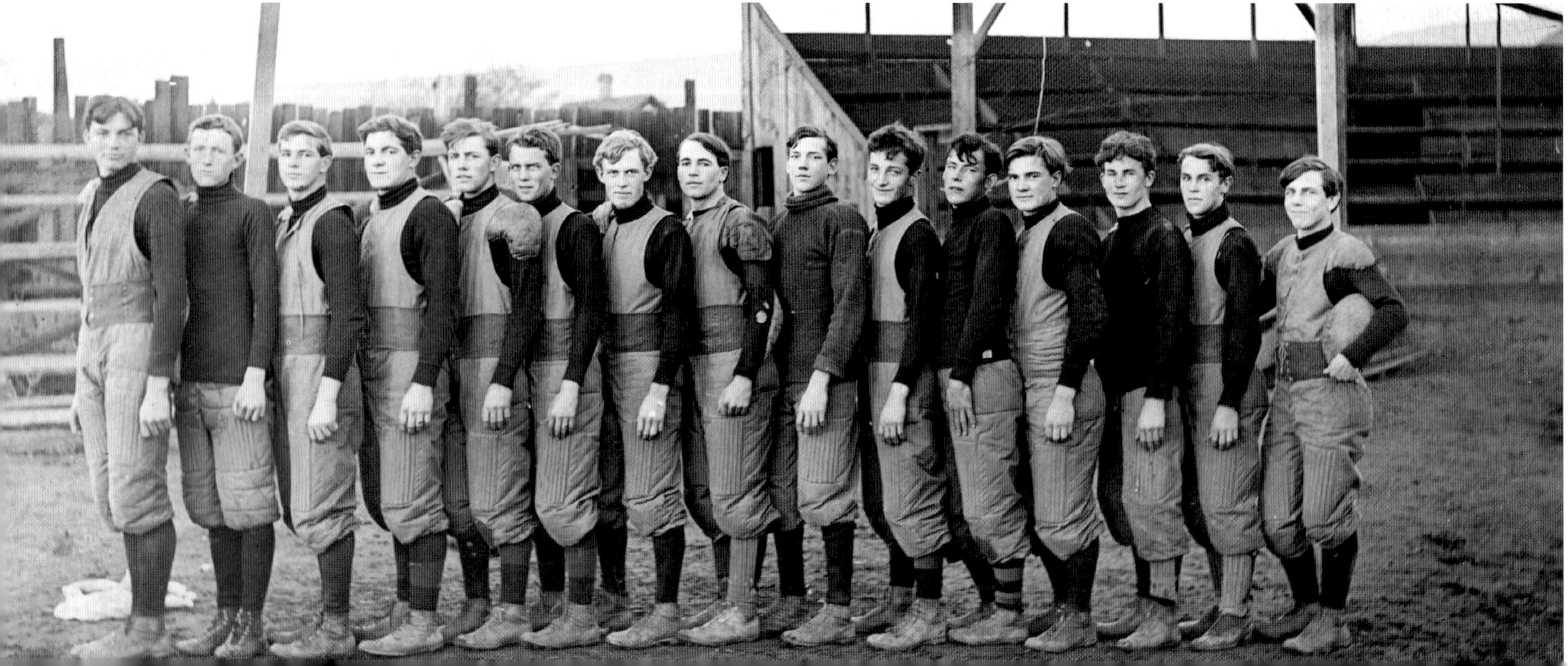

Above: Selah girls playing basketball on the Harrison Place during a Sunday School picnic, circa 1910. *Yakima Valley Museum*

Left: Moxee Central School, circa 1912. *R. MacKintosh*

Below: Nursing school classroom, St. Elizabeth's School of Nursing, North Yakima, circa 1915. *Yakima Valley Museum*

Above: Yakima High School girl students during the summer of 1911.
R. MacKintosh

Left: First school building in the town of Grandview. The building was erected in 1907 and burned in 1924. *Bleyhl Community Library, Grandview*

Right: Girls basketball team, circa 1915.
Yakima Valley Museum

Above: Barge School eighth grade graduation class, 1916. Left to right, top row: Viola Meyers, Velma Wagnon, Georgia Bott, Hazel Baker, Elizabeth Dudley, Anna McLoughlin. Second row: Roland Ward, Pauline Goldberg, Lucilla Dills, Jesse Clark, Eva Knowles, Joseph Gleason, Francis Diem. Sitting: Prescott Tuesley, Ruth Smith, Ruth Clemmer, Martha Turner, Marian Janeck, Doris Inman, Archie Flemming. *Yakima Valley Museum*

Right: Students and teachers posing in front of the Lower Naches High School Building, circa 1918. *Yakima Valley Museum*

Below: Toppenish High School, circa 1915. *Yakima Valley Museum*

Left: Sunnyside High School girls basketball team, 1920. *Yakima Valley Museum*

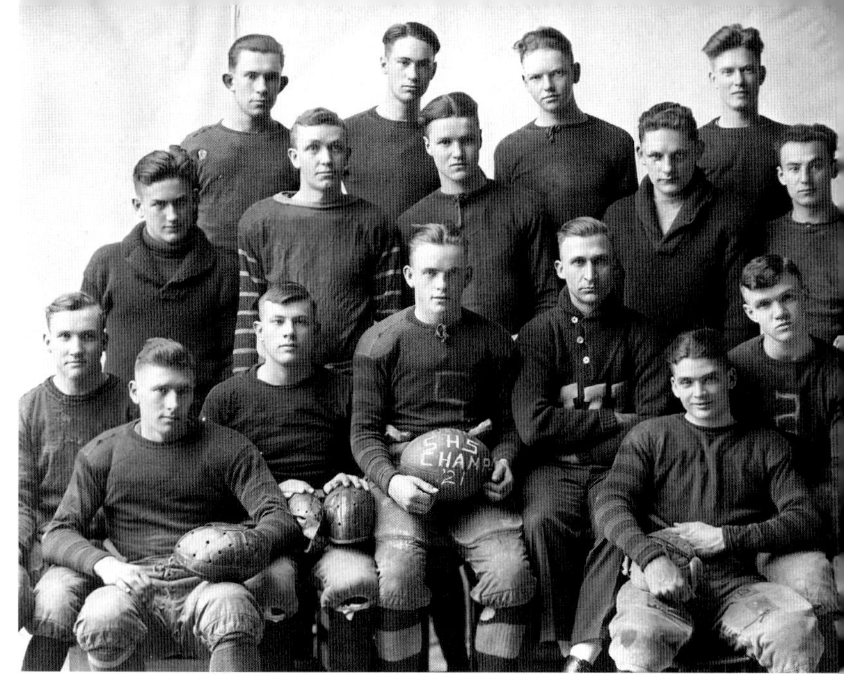

Right: Sunnyside High School boys football team, 1921. *Yakima Valley Museum*

Below: Toppenish High School students, circa 1922. *Yakima Valley Museum*

Above: Miss Alice Scudder taught private kindergarten for many years in Yakima. This picture is the class of 1922. In her first year in North Yakima (1888), Miss Scudder started a collection of wild flowers that is now in the collection at the Smithsonian. *Yakima Valley Museum*

Above Left: Outlook High School basketball team, 1921. Left to right, top row: E.W. Neale, coach; Alfred Fike, "A1"; Lee Laughlin, "Leaky"; Ted Kollmar, "Ted." Bottom row: Russel Price, "Bus"; Clayton McMinnimee, "Spoky"; Dale Wright, "Dot, Pop, Father"; Kenneth Peabody, "Kenny." *Yakima Valley Museum*

Left: Tieton school students pose in front of their school building, 1921. The school was built in 1912 and torn down in 1957. *Yakima Valley Museum*

Above: McKinley Grade School eighth grade graduating class, Yakima, June 7, 1923.

Yakima Valley Museum

Left: Nob Hill School, eighth grade students, Yakima, 1927.

Douglas E. Cowin

Right: North Yakima High School. The school was built in 1908-1909 at Seventh and Walnut, at a cost of $120,000.

Douglas E. Cowin

Below: McKinley School students, 1928. Left to right, First row: Dick Hauser, Walter Smith, Melvin Bailey, Wallace MacIvanie, William Thompson, Harry Renner, Lucas Wisenberger, Sperry Wellons, Gallen Sutton, Lester Harris. Second row: Charles Parkhurst, Ray Beauchamp, Millicent Latta, Richard Green, Eleanor Lewis, Forrest Sainsbury, Margaret Snyder, Allan Perkins, Eva Row, Frank Cliet, Raymond Kumberas. Third row: John Dobrovtch, Eleanor Ham, Forrest Bernath, Elna Lean, Wayne Younger, Elsie Bartram, Nellie Muller, James Glasscock, Margaret Rennie, Maryalice Tomlinson, Esther Thomas, Barbara Bodine, Kenneth Swall, Gwendolyn Longbottom, Robert Spanton. Fourth row: Flavel Silliman, Frances Old, Emma Wert, Gertrude Dowd, Virginia Albrecht, Concordia Munro, Myrtle Fitch, Bessie Ross, Elsie Emerick, Florence Demoray, Dorothy Holtzinger, Lanetta Harrison, Alma Bartram, Dorothy Robinson, Martha Rodenbeck. *Yakima Valley Museum*

GEISEL & PITCHER.
PALACE SHOEING SHOP
A TEXAS RANGER

CHAPTER SEVEN

Community Spirit

If it's true that the heart of a community is in its churches, then the towns of the Yakima Valley demonstrated great heart from their earliest days. Almost as soon as a town's plat was complete — and sometimes even before — the first churches and gathering places were being built.

The tradition began with the mission at Ahtanum, when Catholic priests — "black robes" — recruited by Ka-mi-akin of the Yakama arrived in 1849.

Within 50 years, the list of religious congregations in the Yakima area was lengthy: Congregational, Episcopal, First Baptist, First Methodist, Lutheran, Presbyterian, Roman Catholic, Mennonite, Dunkard and Salvation Army.

By World War I, additions to the religious community included three branches of Lutheran — Swedish, English and German — as well as African Methodist, German Evangelical, Church of God and Nazarene.

The community's spirit also showed in magnificent homes built by the earliest landowners.

Two of the most striking that remain are the Congdon Castle (built by Chester Congdon in about 1914 in an apple orchard between 64th and 72nd avenues on Nob Bill Boulevard) and A.E. Larson's "Rosedell" (with construction started in 1905 and completed in 1909, on West Yakima Avenue).

Left: Dedication and laying of cornerstone of St. Joseph's church at 212 North Fourth Street, North Yakima, 1903. The white Presbyterian Church in the background was used until 1904. *Yakima Valley Museum*

Right: Residence of Hon. Thomas Vance, Yakima, 1890. *Yakima Valley Museum*

Above: Interior of St. Joseph's Catholic Church, Union Gap, circa 1884. Yakima City (now Union Gap). *Yakima Valley Museum*

Left: Oldest standing building in the Yakima Valley. It is known as the Moore-Mattoon cabin and was built in 1865 by Mr. Moore. John P. Mattoon, his wife Martha, and two children, George and Annie, moved into the Moore cabin. John was the farm instructor under Father J.H. Wilbur at Ft. Simcoe in 1864. Martha was the first school teacher in Parker Bottom. *R. MacKintosh*

Below Left: Interior view of a Smohalla's Church, Wanapum, Priest Rapids, circa 1890. *Yakima Valley Regional Library*

Below: Residence of James H. Conrad, Ahtanum,1890. Mr. Conrad was a sheriff of Yakima City. *Yakima Valley Museum*

Left: Prosser residence of Col. Wm. F. Prosser, 1890. *Yakima Valley Museum*

Below Left: St. Joseph's Catholic Church, Yakima City (Union Gap), circa 1896. *Yakima Valley Museum*

Below: Presbyterian Church of Naches. It was erected in the Upper Naches Valley in October 1900 near the foot of the Wenas Grade on land donated by the Selah Ditch Company and Daniel Sinclair, before the platting of the town of Naches in 1906.
Yakima Valley Museum

Right: This church was built as the Methodist Church in 1905 to replace the wood frame building at Third and Chestnut streets in Yakima. The new church cost $40,000. *Yakima Valley Museum*

Below Right: Presbyterian Church at the corner of North Third and A streets, Yakima, 1902. *Yakima Valley Museum*

Below: First Christian Church, Yakima City (Union Gap). Rev. Isaac Flint was the minister. His son, Purdy, donated $500 to build this church and it was dedicated January 1, 1882. *Yakima Valley Museum*

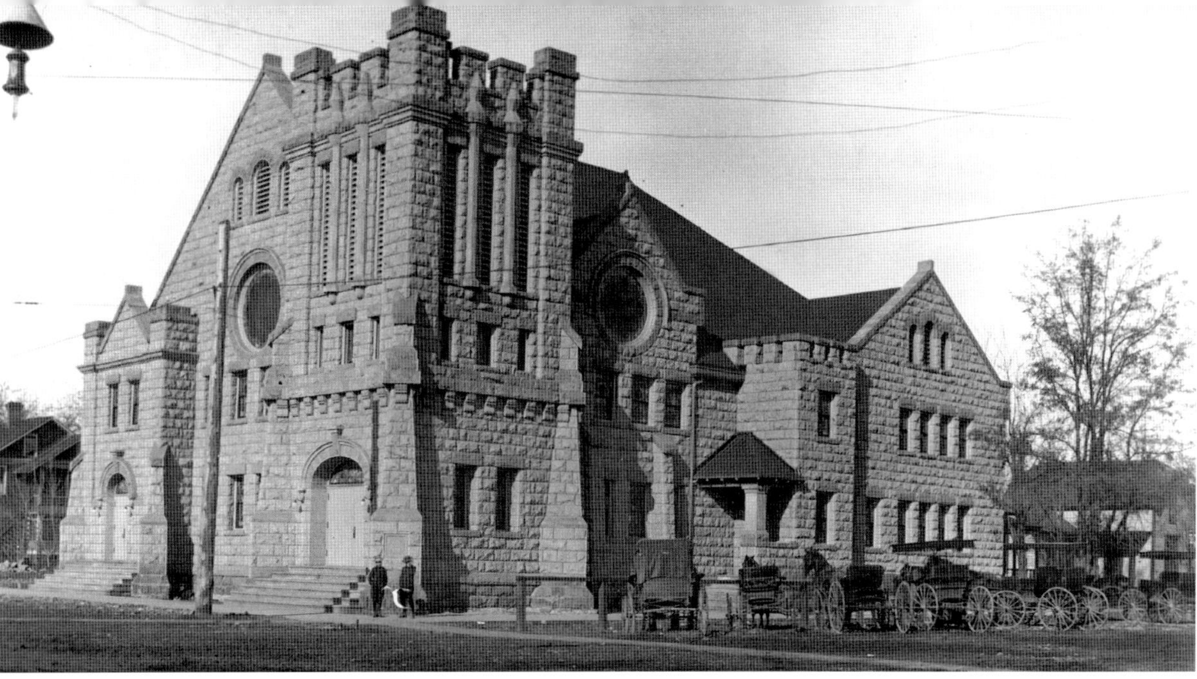

Above: First Baptist Church, Yakima Avenue and North Sixth Street, North Yakima, 1909. The church was dedicated January 10, 1909. *Yakima Valley Museum*

Above Left: Congregational Church between Yakima Avenue and Chestnut on South Third Street, Yakima, circa 1910. The Capitol Theater sits on this lot now. *Yakima Valley Museum*

Left: St. Joseph's Church in the foreground, North Yakima, 1907. The white church in the background was built in 1888 and razed to build Marquette School. *Yakima Valley Museum*

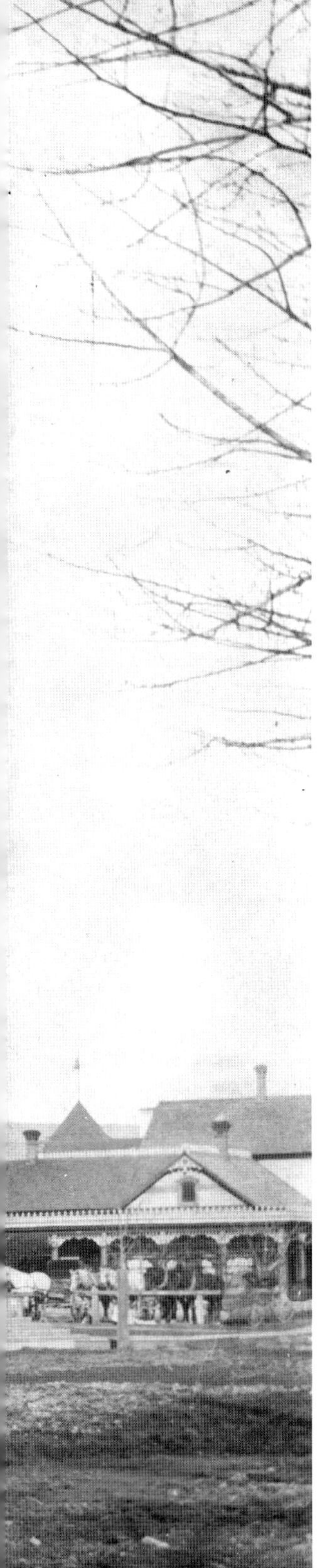

Above: Laying the cornerstone, Bethel African Methodist Episcopal Church, located at 515 South Sixth Street, Yakima, May 22, 1910. *Yakima Valley Museum*

Left: St. Joseph's Catholic Church and rectory at 212 North Fourth Street, North Yakima, circa 1909. *Yakima Valley Museum*

Above Right: Members of the First Christian Church, North Third and B streets, North Yakima, 1909. Pictured are: Mary Bryson, Mrs. E. E. Knowles, Mrs. Julia Van Burskick, Clara G. Yeager, Mrs. P.J. Flint, Celeste L. Harris, D. Evangeline Horwick, Mrs. M.B. Mull, E.E. Knowles, Leon D. Green, H.T. Manning, P.J. Flint, Ralph Harris, F.D. Clemmer, A.L. Flint, M. L. Rose, Perry Yeager, J.A. Adams, F.A. Luse, J.H. Broulette, F.N. Dinger, Dr. Wm. Corpron (?), R.S.Gile, G D. Yeager, W.H. Devaney, Joshep Firidline, D.A.B. Howick, L. Ballinger, Wm. Hedicka, B.F. Young, O.L. Orcutt, Albert Starchen, Geo. Barlow, L.D. Luce, J.E. Fitch, James Ritchie, W.A. Shippert, J.J. Odes, A.B. Pearson, Harry Ingham, A.E. Rasmussen. *Yakima Valley Museum*

Above: Presbyterian Church congregation in front of their church in North Yakima, circa 1912. *Yakima Valley Museum*

Above: Ground breaking for the Masonic Temple at North Fourth and Yakima avenues, North Yakima, September 10, 1910. *Yakima Valley Museum*

Right: Construction of the Masonic Temple at the corner of North Fourth and Yakima avenues, North Yakima, circa 1911. *Yakima Valley Museum*

Below: The "What" Social in the social banquet room of the new First Christian Church, circa 1909. About 125 people attended the "What" social, the first of a series of socials for the boys of the congregation. *Yakima Valley Museum*

Above: Bethany Presbyterian Church in Grandview, circa 1912. *Bleyhl Community Library, Grandview*

Left Above: First Christian Church congregation in front of their church at North Third and B streets, North Yakima. The church was built in 1908. *Yakima Valley Museum*

Below: Roland Brown residence at 617 Fifth Avenue South, Yakima, circa 1914. *Stephanie Brown*

Right and Below: The main barn on the Congdon Orchard property west Nob Hill Boulevard, Yakima, 1912-1920. *Patrick & Aleatha Ehmer*

Left: Construction crew working on the Congdon Castle takes time to pose for a photo, North Yakima, circa 1913. The Castle has 80 rooms and a swimming pool in the basement. *Patrick & Aleatha Ehmer*

Below Left: A view of Congdon Castle under construction, circa 1913. *Patrick & Aleatha Ehmer*

Below: Interior of the entrance hallway of Congdon Castle while it was under construction, circa 1913. *Patrick & Aleatha Ehmer*

Above Left: Construction workers at Congdon Castle, circa 1913. *Patrick & Aleatha Ehmer*

Above: Congdon Castle indoor pool, circa 1916. *Patrick & Aleatha Ehmer*

Left: Congdon Castle nearing completion, circa 1915. *Patrick & Aleatha Ehmer*

Right: Overview of Congdon Castle showing orchards and Interurban Trolley lines in foreground, circa 1920. *Yakima Valley Museum*

Above: First Presbyterian Church located at North Third Street and A, North Yakima, circa 1900. Y.M.C.A. is on the left. *Douglas E. Cowin*

Right: Indian M.E. Church. Original Father Wilbur Memorial Methodist Church. Built in 1879, burned in 1937. *Yakima Valley Museum*

Below Right: First Christian Church board and members in front of the church at Third and B streets, Yakima, 1940. The church was built in 1908. *Douglas E. Cowin*

Above: Nazarene Camp Meeting at the State Fair Grounds, Yakima, July 19-29, 1923. *Yakima Valley Museum*

Left: First Presbyterian Church on West Yakima Avenue and South Eighth Avenue, Yakima, 1940s. *Yakima Valley Museum*

Below: Pioneer Day celebration at the Old St. Joseph Mission, Ahtanum, July 1923. The mission was first established in 1847 by missionary priests Charles Pandosy, Casmir Chirouse and George Blanchet. It is located along the creek at the base of Ahtanum Ridge, 15 miles southwest of the present-day downtown Yakima. It was near the home of Yakama Chief Ka-mi-akin, in what was then the Oregon Territory. *Yakima Valley Museum*

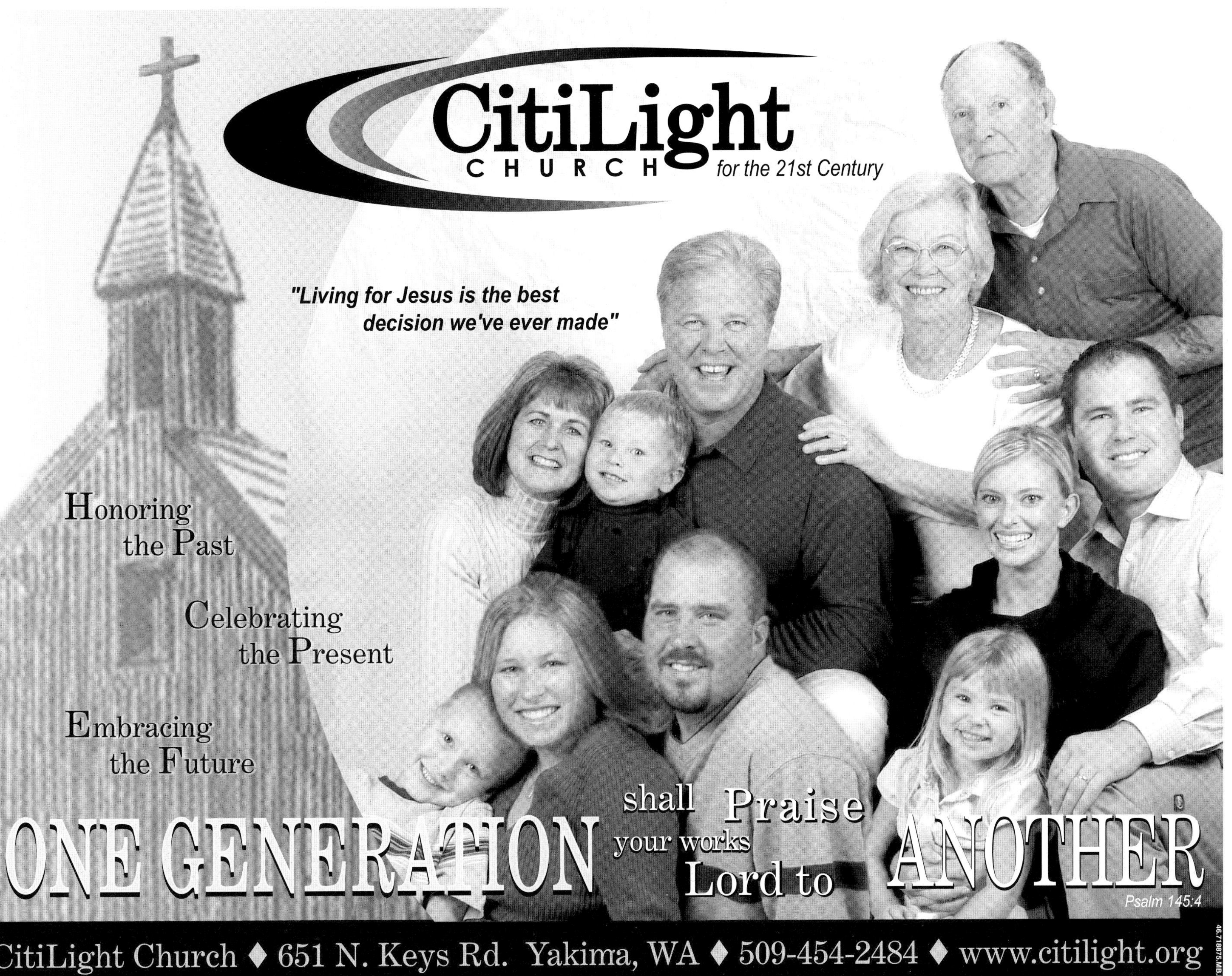
CitiLight
CHURCH
for the 21st Century
"Living for Jesus is the best
decision we've ever made"
Honoring
the Past
Celebrating
the Present
Embracing
the Future
ONE GENERATION
shall Praise
your works
Lord to
ANOTHER
Psalm 145:4
CitiLight Church ♦ 651 N. Keys Rd. Yakima, WA ♦ 509-454-2484 ♦ www.citilight.org

EL SYDNEY

CHAPTER EIGHT

Tradition of Public Service

When the U.S. Army built Fort Simcoe near White Swan on the Yakama Reservation in 1856, it was the beginning of what would become a tradition of public and military service in the Yakima Valley.

The Washington State National Guard Company of North Yakima was organized as a cavalry unit, but was allowed to serve as infantry in order to muster for the war against Spain in 1898. But the 109 men of Company E, First Washington Volunteer Infantry would see duty not in Cuba against the Spanish, but rather in the Philippines against Filipino nationalists. Ten local soldiers and one nurse were killed in battles in February and March 1899 before the company was mustered out. They were the Valley's first war dead. They would not be the last.

Protection was also needed in the burgeoning and lusty towns throughout the Valley, which in the 1880s were populated with few families and many single workmen, many of whom had arrived with the railroad.

But as the 19th century turned and the towns were tamed, police forces, firefighting and postal service were established throughout the Yakima Valley.

Left: Horse drawn fire engine with crew at station located at 21 North Front Street, Yakima, circa 1909. Seated is Gus Perkins with reins in hand, Ed Dawson next to him. Standing is McKinney Dow Lambert with Checkers (large dog) and Tiny (small dog). Next to him is Chas. Coombs, R.L. Bucklin and Jeff Hoker. This building still stands. *Yakima Valley Museum*

Right: Two members of the Yakima County Sheriffs Department's "Dry Squad" during prohibition, circa 1930. *Yakima Valley Museum*

Eleventh Annual Encampment, Grand Army of the Republic, June 14-15, 1893, North Yakima

1 – Charles Dodge, North Yakima
2 – D W Stair. North Yakima
3 – E Parmentier, Norman
4 – J F McLean, Walla Walla
5 – T M Young, Seattle
6 – Unidentified
7 – C M Price, Centralia
8 – A J Smith, Asst Adj Gen, Spokane
9 – Master Jimmie Watson Spokane
10 – J L Brown, Dept Com, Spokane
11 – A H H Cowgar, Ellensburgh
12 – Unidentified
13 – A J Lewis, North Yakima
14 – Byron Phelps, Seattle
15 – George Kinnear, Seattle
16 – R S Morgan, North Yakima
17 – George Klock, North Yakima
18 – J B McMillan, Port Townsend
19 – G H Boardman, Tacoma
20 – J W Young, North Yakima
21 – M P Kelly, Tacoma
22 – P S Burke, North Yakima
23 – J W Langley, Seattle
24 – James Leddy, Seattle
25 – C S Eichholtz, Tacoma
26 – L D Rodgers, Orting
27 – W F Taylor, Tacoma
28 – B B Brownson, Tacoma
29 – M F Keenon, North Yakima
30 – M Ward, North Yakima
31 – C P Wakeman, Port Townsend
32 – Robert Scott, North Yakima
33 – Captain Robert Dunn, North Yakima
34 – _____ Baker, North Yakima
35 – I J Lichtenberg, Seattle
36 – F M Hanson, Seattle
37 – Captain E C Curtis, Puyallup
38 – E R Leaming, North Yakima
39 – Unidentified
40 – George Bonner, North Yakima
41 – M M Holmes, Past Dept Com, Seattle
42 – Unidentified
43 – W L Whittemore, Kent
44 – H S Lillagar, S V C, Orting
45 – _____ Wommick, Bickleton
46 – J S Watson, Spokane
47 – J Conaway, Ballard
48 – J F Sinclari, Com Elect, Ballard
49 – Walter J Reed, Cle-Elum
50 – J P McCafferty, North Yakima
51 – N H Yeates, North Yakima
52 – Jesse Tobias, Excelsior
53 – J J Moss, Chaplain, Seattle
54 – J B Clark, Madrone
55 – C H Holmes, Tacoma
56 – J M Henderson, North Yakima
57 – E Burton, La Conner
58 – George Hart, Auburn
59 – J T Whorton, North Yakima
60 – Unidentified
61 – G W Gardner, North Yakima
62 – F H Hurd, Seattle
63 – N R Bissell, Auburn
64 – J K Ward, North Yakima
65 – John Gagman, La Conner
66 – Mike Ferrell, North Yakima
67 – Unidentified
68 – Henry A Nordeck, North Yakima
69 – J F Dwelley, La Conner
70 – Unidentified
71 – R S Alexander, Excelsior
72 – James Gleed, North Yakima
73 – A J Crookham, Spokane
74 – James Monroe, North Yakima
75 – George B Lane
76 – R B Scott, Spokane
77 – C T Patterson, S V C elect, Excelsior
78 – Col W F Prosser, North Yakima
81 – A V Fawcett, Tacoma
82 – John G Broyle, New Whatcom
83 – S J Lowe, North Yakima
84 – M N Mansfield, North Yakima
85 – R W Smith, Yakima City
86 – Thad S Smith, Port Townsend
87 – F S Davis, North Yakima
88 – Isaac Hayes, North Yakima
89 – John Leason, North Yakima
90 – J M Beamiss, Seattle
91 – W G Simpson, Prosser
92 – William Phillips, Seattle
93 – F M Davis, Seattle
94 – Thomas M Fisher, Port Townsend
95 – J N Scott, Port Townsend
96 – Unidentified
97 – T C Hopkins, Seattle
98 – C D Oyley, Seattle
99 – James H Wilson, Seattle
100 – J W McDowell, Ellensburgh
101 – J L Conn, Tacoma
102 – G H Brock, Seattle
103 – L A Treen, Seattle
104 – Daniel Winter, Auburn
105 – Robert Van Buskirk, North Yakima
106 – I L Burton, Ellensburgh
107 – B C Bedell, Walla Walla
108 – Edward Rose, Port Townsend
109 – Joseph Hawkins, Yakima City
110 – A S Paul, North Yakima
111 – Monroe Daggett, St. Mary's Idaho
112 – B B Coombs, North Yakima
113 – Unidentified
114 – J O Clark, North Yakima
115 – Sam F Haines, North Yakima
116 – Unidentified
117 – J P Dorfen, Ross
118 – J G Curtis, Centralia
119 – L C Lovell, North Yakima
120 – W M F Wallace, J V C elect, South Bend
121 – John Convrey, Seattle
122 – George W Tibbetts, Gillman
123 – W W Perrigo, Seattle
124 – J C Adams, Ritzville
125 – S F Street, Orting
126 – Don G Lovell, Tacoma
127 – D Coiner, Seattle

Above: First Tieton Post Office and General Store, with dance hall upstairs, circa 1907.
Yakima Valley Museum

Above Left: A group of men in front of Yakima County Courthouse for an auction of Yakima Investment Company's property, March 5, 1900. The Courthouse burned, May 5, 1906. *Yakima Valley Museum*

Left: Cowiche Post Office and Store with a group of men and wagons in foreground, early 1900s.
Yakima Valley Museum

RURAL
DELIVERY
ROUTE
1
U.S.

Above: North Yakima Police force, on Taft Day, September 29, 1909. Left to right, top row: Matt Staniger, Art Kinyon, W.D. Walter, Lorenzo Walters, James Ferris, Walter Pettyjohn, B.H. Hogan, Jack Gilmore, Asa Peck. Bottom row: Jake Elmore ____Wakefield, Frank Looker, O.B. Grant, Bob Mathews, Tom Story (chief of police), Frank Millican, Ed Sanders, Charley Niles, Howard Taylor, Mack Kinnerman (second chief). *Yakima Valley Museum*

Left: Rural mail carrier, Mabton, 1907. *Yakima Valley Museum*

Right: Firemen harnessing horses for a call by dropping the harness from above by ropes, North Yakima, circa 1907. Left to right: Chief Dawson, A.L. Bucklin, Charles Coombs, McKinney Dow Lambert, Gus Perkins. *Yakima Valley Museum*

Above and Left: Local National Guard unit, circa 1910. *Elizabeth Irons*

Right: First motorized fire engine in North Yakima, a 1907 Dart Apparatus, at Front Street Station in the Opera House Building, circa 1907. Notice the steering wheel on the right side of the fire engine. *Yakima Valley Museum*

HOSE NO. 2

Above Left: New Webb Motor Fire Engine at the station at Third and Walnut, streets, North Yakima, circa 1914. *Yakima Valley Museum*

Above Right: Auto fire department, North Yakima, 1912. It was known as the only complete motorized fire department west of the Mississippi at the time. *Yakima Valley Museum*

Left: Yakima County Court House, circa 1912. The statue of Col. Weisenberger was moved from Yakima Avenue and Third Street to the Courthouse lawn. It was erected in memory of the fallen of Company E of the 1st Regiment of the Washington U.S. Volunteer Infantry, 1898-1899. The monument is now at Yakima Avenue and Naches Avenue. *Yakima Valley Museum*

Right: Yakima County Sheriff's car and driver, circa 1912. Notice the right hand steering wheel. *Yakima Valley Museum*

Above: North Yakima Fire Department chemical truck, steamer and crew in front of Fire Station No. 2 at 16 North Fourth Avenue in North Yakima, circa 1914. *Yakima Valley Museum*

Right: All motorized fire engines on display in front of station at South Third and Walnut streets in North Yakima, circa 1913. *Yakima Valley Museum*

Left: Exterior of the Fire Department Headquarters at South Third and Walnut streets, North Yakima, with trucks in foreground, circa 1914. *Yakima Valley Museum*

Above: St. Elizabeth's Hospital on South Ninth Avenue, North Yakima, circa 1915. *Yakima Valley Museum*

Above: National Guard maneuvers at the Louis F. Hart Camp, 1915. *Karen Harvey*

Below: Company C, 2nd Infantry, National Guard, Yakima, 1915. *Karen Harvey*

The Old Warehouse

705 Railroad Avenue
In Downtown Zillah
Easy Access Off I-82 • Exit 52 or 54
509/829-5700

Open Mon-Sat.
9:30 - 5:30
Closed Sunday

The Old Warehouse. Not that the name has much to do with what's inside, because once you get inside the vast 45,000 square ft. of furniture, you're bowled over by the contents of the establishment. There are huge carved sleigh beds & matching bureaus, sofas of every description, dining sets, framed prints & posters, lamps, end tables & life-sized human statues. Over 50 truck loads of furniture.

Plan on having a pleasant shopping experience while at the same time saving a great deal of money on your new furniture and mattresses.

The old Perham cold storage warehouse has a lot of memories, and was one of Zillah's earliest industries. The new owners have enjoyed the many stories from people who have either worked or done business at the old warehouse.

Then & Now

The new owners have done extensive remodeling throughout the entire building, including a sprinkler system and a beautiful 6,000 ft. deck. The second story still has a convenient entrance. Trucks used to back up to the rear entrance and a large machine would "lift" the load off and transport it upstairs to the loft. They left the 'cold storage' tubes in place, which kept the temperatures at about 32-33 degrees.

We have a large selection of leather & oak furniture.

Washington's most unique & fun furniture store.

Above: Fire department equipment lined up in front of main station at South Third and Walnut streets, North Yakima, circa 1923. *Yakima Valley Museum*

Left: Washington State Auditors and Treasurer's Convention, Yakima, September 14-15, 1923. Photo was taken on the steps of the Courthouse. *Yakima Valley Museum*

Opposite: Two Washington State Patrol officers with motorcycles, circa 1930. *Yakima Valley Museum*

Below: William "Bill" Wharton, right, and Harry Eddy returning from World War I, circa 1919. *Karen Harvey*

PATROL
8028
HIGHWAY
PATROL
WN
E-30 8058

CHAPTER NINE

PEOPLE OF THE VALLEY

The Longmire wagon train of 1853 was the first of its kind to enter the Yakima Valley, not with the idea of settling but just seeking a shorter route to the Puget Sound.

Some of the Longmire party, however, remembered the beauty and possibility of the Valley and returned to Yakima to make their homes.

They were only the first of the immigrants to arrive.

The lands for hundreds of generations had already been home to the First People, what would eventually become known as the Yakama Nation. It would take the Indian Wars of 1855-56 before the two peoples could share the land.

The white men continued to come, drawn by promises of free homestead land and bountiful harvests.

In 1880, the population of Yakima County was just 2,811. (It was a sign of the times that only the white population was counted in the Census.) That grew nearly fivefold in the next decade, to a population of 13,206 in 1890.

Other immigrants followed — from all over the United States, and from France, Germany, Norway, Japan, the Philippines and Mexico, to name just a few of the nationalities throughout the Valley.

The most recent Census, from the year 2000, shows the county's population at 225,000.

Left: American Indian children, 1910. *Yakima Valley Museum*

Right: Collier and Dopps families pose for this photograph in Granger, 1912. *Karen Harvey*

CELEBRATING OUR HERITAGE

509/965-6655 • 3911 CASTLEVALE ROAD, STE. 209
WWW.WINDERMERE.COM

Windermere is happy to join in this photographic celebration capturing the history in our community. Working together, we can ensure that in future years, the quality of life in Yakima we've come to appreciate will be here for generations to come.

46.718350.YMB.F

Above: Chief White Swan of the Yakama Nation and his wife pose with George and Eliza Waters, circa 1900. George Waters was an regularly ordained minister in the Columbia River Conference.
Yakima Valley Museum

Left: Yakama women pose for the photographer, circa 1910. *Yakima Valley Museum*

Right: Portrait of Charley Thompson, a Yakama cowboy, circa 1900. *Yakima Valley Regional Library*

Above: Francis Thola family in their 1908 International car. Left to right, seated in front is Lawrence. First row: Father Francis, Frank and Henry. Second row: Anna, Elizabeth and Mother Elizabeth and John. The Thola family came from Bancroft, Iowa, in 1911 and made their home at what is now 40th and Summitview avenues where they had a fruit ranch. Later they bought acreage west on Summitview and 88th where they continued to raise apples and soft fruit and operated their own warehouse. *Arlene M. Cuillier*

Above: Josiah and Rachael Rowen, circa 1910. Josiah was a Civil War vet with Company C, 14 Regimental Pennsylvania Volunteers. *Stephanie Brown*

Left: Charles Hess on right, the other unidentified, Yakima, circa 1910.
Elizabeth Irons

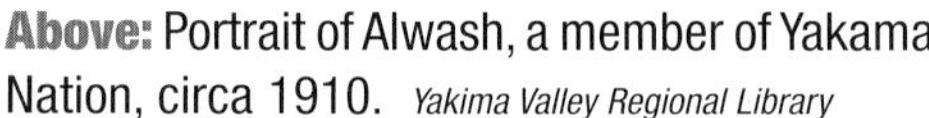

Above: Portrait of Alwash, a member of Yakama Nation, circa 1910. *Yakima Valley Regional Library*

Above Middle: Earl Hecox, circa 1910. *Joseph Hecox*

Above Right: Family photo, Wood, Woods and Beckes, 1911. Left to right, back row: Mr. Woods and son, Charlie Wood, Richard B. Beckes, Charlie Tharp, Lillian G. Beckes holding Lillian (King), Orson Beckes, Oliver Beckes holding Richard Beckes, Edwin Beckes. Middle row: Mrs. Woods and daughter, Sadie Woods, Edwin Woods, Ella Beckes, Alice Beckes Tharp, Ethel (Mains) Beckes. Bottom row: Charlotte Tharp, Marguerite Beckes, Helen Beckes, Ione Woods, Robert Beckes, Laura Tharp, Muriel Beckes, Lloyd Beckes. *Yakima Valley Museum*

Right: William and Reinsek Oord family, Zillah, 1911. *Norma Friend*

Left: Jack Ambrose hunting in the fall of 1915. *R. MacKintosh*

Below Left: Derk and Augusta Oord Omta, Zillah, 1923. *Norma Friend*

Below: The children of John and Ella Lynch, circa 1921. The children's name, clockwise beginning with the baby: Betty, Geraldine, Dorothy, Francis, Pauline. *Joseph Hecox*

Left: Wedding photo of Ray and Laura Hecox, Yakima, September 6, 1920. *Joseph Hecox*

Right: Wray Brown with his parents Roland and Emma Brown, circa 1930. Wray Brown founded Wray's Market.
Stephanie Brown

Below: The wedding party and family of Florence Ditter (bride) of Yakima and George Corbett (groom) by St. Joseph Church where they were married, 1932.
Christine Corbett Conklin

Above: Dr. Delmar F. Bice, M.D., 1935. For 30 days Dr. Bice made his house calls on horseback as part of Yakima's Golden Jubilee. This photo made several newspapers including the Los Angeles Times. *Del Bice*

Above Left: Celebrating Golden Jubilee by growing beards in Yakima, 1935, are Earl and Ray Hecox with their father Fred. *Joseph Hecox*

Left: Rod MacKintosh poses in front of his father's car at the Yakima Valley Junior College (formerly Columbia School) on Fourth Avenue, Yakima, circa 1937. *R. MacKintosh*

Above: Oord family photo, 1937. *Norma Friend*

Left: Three future May Queens, Rosella Bragstad (Brown), Jean Rankin and Barbara Rankin,1920s. *Stephanie Brown*

Left Below: Elsie Cowin hunting rabbits in Wapato, circa 1910. *Douglas E. Cowin*

Below: Elsie and Earle Cowin at the train station, circa 1905. *Douglas E. Cowin*

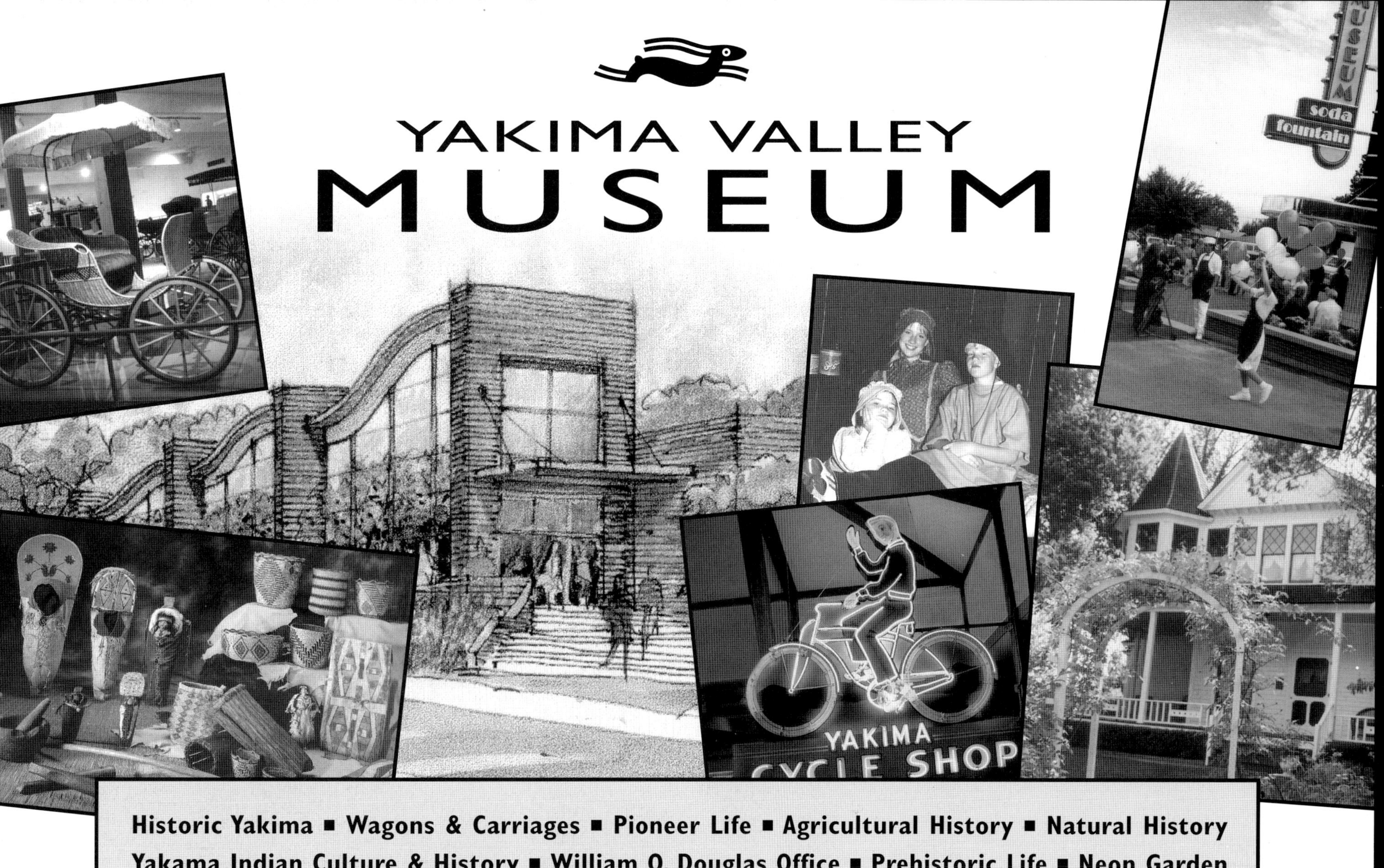
YAKIMA VALLEY
MUSEUM
MUSEUM
soda
fountain
YAKIMA
CYCLE SHOP

PIONEER DRUG CO.
DRUGS
THE REXALL STORE
WATCHES

CHAPTER TEN

RECREATION & CELEBRATION

It didn't take long for the nascent communities of the Yakima Valley to begin celebrating their existence. The party began with statehood in 1889 and continued with Pioneer Days, Blossom Festivals, Fourth of Julys and every sort of civic celebration.

Two of the biggest celebrations were for visits to Yakima by presidents of the United States — Theodore Roosevelt in 1903 and William Taft in 1909.

And with the parties came music from a wide variety of community bands, including the North Yakima Cornet Band as early as 1905.

There were also celebrations for winning sports teams, with football and baseball early (and continuing) favorites. And as soon as there were automobiles in the Valley, there was auto racing at the Washington State Fair. The fair itself has been a tradition since 1894. (It was reorganized and renamed the Central Washington State Fair in 1939.)

In between those big events, townspeople were finding other types of recreation — the number and popularity of first, theatrical productions, and later, movies, grew, the Yakima County Club was developed not long after that and paved roads led to more visiting and travel throughout the Valley.

Left: Blossom Festival, Yakima, 1913. *Yakima Valley Museum*

Right: Mason's Opera House, North First Street, 1890. Janeck's Pharmacy was located on the first floor. *Yakima Valley Museum*

Above: North Yakima Cornet Band members, circa 1905.
Yakima Valley Museum

Right: J.V. Payne and his North Yakima baseball team, circa 1900.
Yakima Valley Museum

Below: Picnic at Eschbach ranch, Yakima, early 1900. At the park there were picnic tables, dance floor, boat rides, swimming and ice cream. *Christine Corbett Conklin*

Above: President Theodore Roosevelt speaks from a train during his visit to Yakima May 25, 1903. *Yakima Valley Museum*

Above Left: President Roosevelt's Parade at intersection of Yakima Avenue and First Street, May 25, 1903. *Yakima Valley Museum*

Left: President Roosevelt's Parade down Yakima Avenue, May 25, 1903. *Yakima Valley Museum*

Opposite and Right: President William Taft speaks at North Yakima from the Courthouse steps, September 29, 1909. *Yakima Valley Museum*

Below: North Yakima Juvenile Band, pose for the photograph on the steps of the Courthouse 1909. Nagler was the conductor. *Alma Harris*

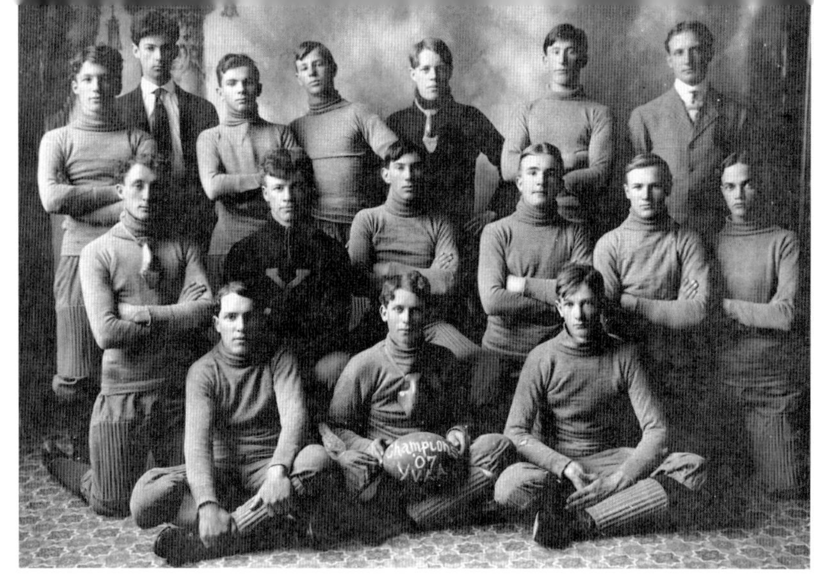

Above: Football champions, 1907. Yakima Valley Athletic Association.

Yakima Valley Museum

Above Right: Little Oakland $1,000 car going a good mile on the state race track in North Yakima, 1910.

Yakima Valley Museum

Right: Zillah Concert Band at Granger, circa 1910. *Yakima Valley Museum*

Above: View of the Mabton Hay Palace during the Hay Palace Fair, circa 1910. *Yakima Valley Museum*

Left: Selah Baseball Club of 1911. *Yakima Valley Museum*

Below: Fourth of July parade, Wiley City, 1912. Wiley City was named by Hugh Wiley, an early pioneer. *Yakima Valley Museum*

Above: Blossom Festival, North Yakima, 1912. *Christine Corbett Conklin*

Opposite page: View of the Washington State Fair, North Yakima, circa 1912. The Horticulture Building, built in 1894, and still standing, can be seen at the right. *Yakima Valley Museum*

Below: Blossom Festival, North Yakima, 1912. Congdon Orchards float is advertising 35,000 apple and pear trees. *Christine Corbett Conklin*

RIGATION.

Above: Family picnic at Soda Springs at the North Fork of the Ahtanum, circa 1918. Soda Springs was the vacation spot for early pioneers. *Patrick & Aleatha Ehmer*

Below: Queen of the Blossom Festival, North Yakima, 1912. *Christine Corbett Conklin*

Above: Blossom Festival parade, May 1913. The parade is going west on Yakima Avenue. *Yakima Valley Museum*

Left: Boat landing, Sumach Park, North Yakima, circa 1915. Sumach Park was a park on the Yakima River until it was washed out during a flood. *Douglas E. Cowin*

Below: Blossom Festival, Yakima, 1913. *Yakima Valley Museum*

Above: A large group of children participating in the "Learn to Swim Week" at the Natatorium in North Yakima, circa 1914. *Yakima Valley Regional Library*

Above: World War I parade going west on Yakima Avenue, Yakima, circa 1917. *Yakima Valley Museum*

Left: Pool players at the Front Street Saloon, Yakima, circa 1920. *Yakima Valley Museum*

Right: Armistice Day Parade at Third Street and East Yakima Avenue, Yakima, 1922. In the front is Doris Hillyard. Left is Betty Brush (Elizabeth). Right is Carolyn Brush and center back is Helen Hardy.

Joanna Frisque

Below: Second Annual Speed Classic, Yakima, May 31, 1926.

Yakima Valley Museum

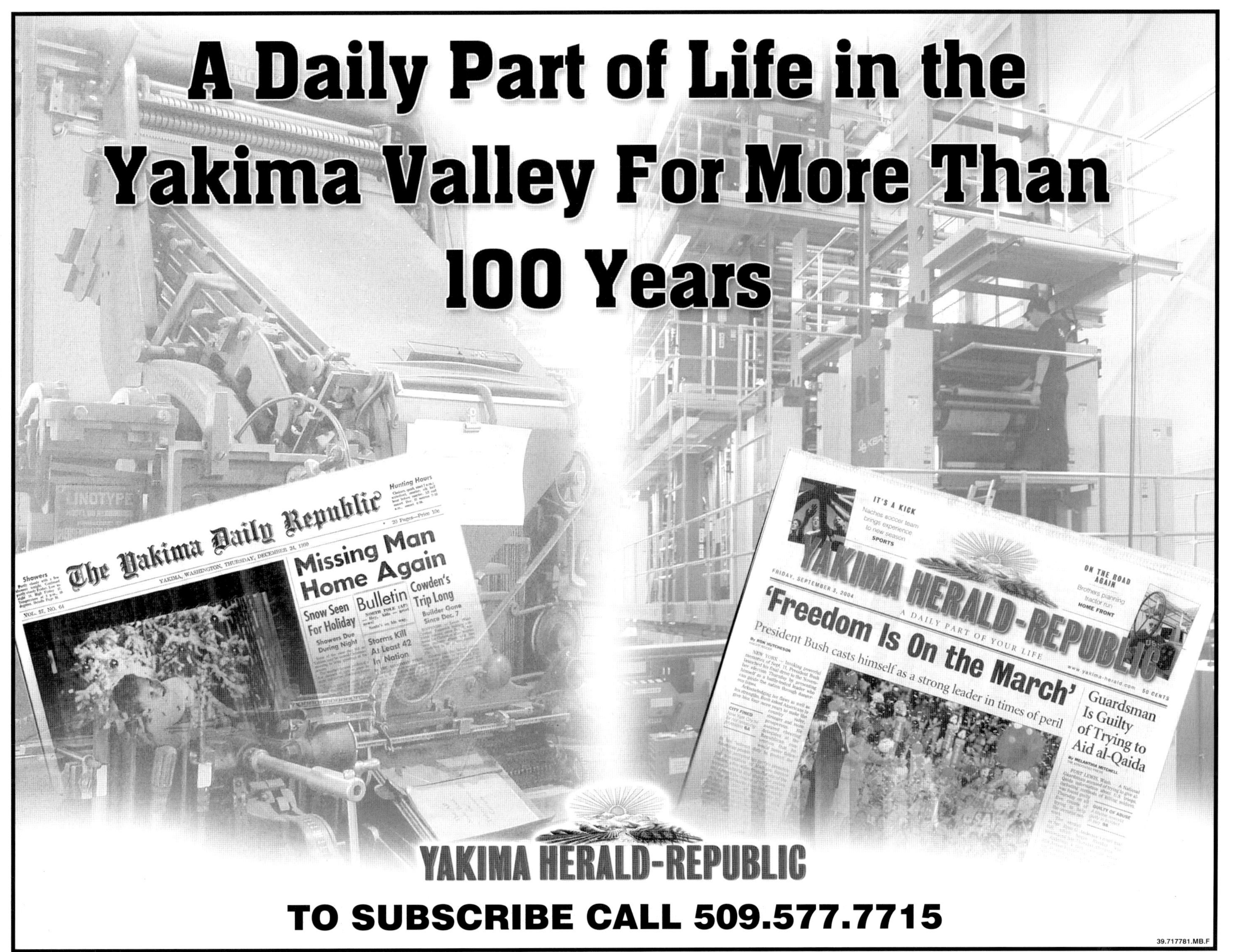

A Daily Part of Life in the Yakima Valley For More Than 100 Years
The Yakima Daily Republic
Missing Man Home Again
Bulletin
Cowden's Trip Long
Snow Seen For Holiday
Storms Kill At Least 42 In Nation
YAKIMA HERALD-REPUBLIC
A DAILY PART OF YOUR LIFE
'Freedom Is On the March'
President Bush casts himself as a strong leader in times of peril
Guardsman Is Guilty of Trying to Aid al-Qaida
YAKIMA HERALD-REPUBLIC
TO SUBSCRIBE CALL 509.577.7715
39.717781.MB.F

Above: Paradise Valley Camp Ground, Tatoosh Range in the background, circa 1920. *Yakima Valley Museum*

Above: Start of an automobile race at Washington State Fairgrounds in Yakima, 1927. *Yakima Valley Museum*

Below: Group of men gather for a photo during the Golden Jubilee, which celebrated the city of Yakima's 50th anniversary in 1935. Identified in the photo: W.W. deVeaux, Alex Corbett, Ed Linberg, W. N. Irish, Warren White, Dr. Berg, ____Whitmer, Herman Loevinstein, Ellery van Diest, Jack Evans, Zeb Kinsey, Walter Traub, Elmer Wilcox, Henry Rodenback, John Smith, Reid Thomas, D. O.G. Chisholm, George Euler, Lincoln Shoeshine, Leslie Rose, Erwin Howard, Winfield Boyd, GOD. Acquisition, Walter Theme, Ed Rankin, Charles Stockdale, Frank Sears, Charles Carpenter, Lawrence Wharton, Dick Dibbling, Roy Conklin, Stanley Veliekanje, W.S. Holt, Ben Tidlund, Charles Russell, Dell Fleming, Walter Weaver, Jake Guns, Dick Thome, Roy Hodge, Gilbert Hall, Roy Brown, George Weber, Chester Miller, Joe Thorndyke, ____Bacon, Hollis Cowell, Ray Hare. *Yakima Valley Museum*

Above: Pioneer Days celebration in Yakima, 1937. *Yakima Valley Museum*

All Above: Yakima's Golden Jubilee Celebration in 1935. *R. MacKintosh*

Left: Group of men pose with a car beside the clubhouse at the Yakima Country Club in the 1930s.
Yakima Valley Museum

Above: YMCA located at Fourth Street and Yakima Avenue, North Yakima, circa 1925. *Douglas E. Cowin*

Right: The Pix Theater in Toppenish, circa 1941. *Yakima Valley Museum*

Below: Crowd in line at the Roxy Theater located at 7 East Yakima Avenue, Yakima, 1936. *Yakima Valley Museum*